If we really believed that it is more blessed to give than to receive (Acts 20:35), we would not ask, 'How much do I have to give?' but, 'How much can I give?' In this much-needed book, Joel Morris shows us that a generous heart is the happiest heart, for it aims to imitate and glorify God.

JOEL R. BEEKE
President, Puritan Reformed Theological Seminary, Grand
Rapids, Michigan

This little book packs a big punch. Joel Morris starts by showing us the enormity of God's generosity to us in the gospel, and that the only proper response is our own cheerful and open-handed generosity. He uses heart-warming illustrations to show us practically what this looks like, but he also challenges us to self-examination to understand what type of giver we are. This is a book that lifts our vision to heaven to see the all-generous God, and then urges us on to respond to this with a radical generosity towards the local church and fuelling gospel work. A must-read for all believers but particularly for those of us who have a tendency to forget that all that we have and enjoy is God's and not our own.

SIMON PILLAR
Managing Director of Pacific Equity Partners (PEP)
A Founder of the Gospel Patrons movement

The love of God spills out of the pages of *Big Hearted*. Joel Morris' beautiful work will inspire you to ask God to conform you into His image – namely that of a cheerful, sacrificial, generous, loving, and big-hearted giver. Read, apply, and rejoice.

CHUCK BENTLEY
CEO, Crown.org & Author, *7 Gray Swans, Trends That Threaten Our Financial Future*

BIG
HEARTED

Forewords by Dr. Michael Reeves and Daryl Heald

BIG
HEARTED

Are You Giving Happily
or Hesitantly?

JOEL MORRIS

Copyright © Joel Morris 2021

hardback ISBN 978-1-5271-0698-7
ebook ISBN 978-1-5271-0785-4

10 9 8 7 6 5 4 3 2 1

Published in 2021
by
Christian Focus Publications, Ltd.
Geanies House, Fearn,
Ross-shire, IV20 1TW, Scotland.
www.christianfocus.com

Cover design by Pete Barnsley

Printed by Gutenberg, Malta

CONTENTS

To my dear wife Hye Lim.
You are the most generous person I know!

Foreword
by Michael Reeves

This book is not a harangue or a guilt trip. It's more like a holiday in the Caribbean for the soul: it refreshes you in the gospel so that you come away warmed and energized by the sheer kindness of God. It is a book especially good for anyone whose Christian life feels flat, anyone going through the motions of being Christian without true happiness in God.

I've had the fun of working with Dr. Joel Morris for a number of years now, and I keep finding myself impressed by his benevolence and his heart for the gospel. It is that heart that shines through here. More, we see the reason for it: the goodness of God that stirs his heart.

We hear all too much these days about hypocrisy in the church and a lack of integrity in her leaders. My burning desire as we raise up leaders across the world in Union School of Theology is that we might cultivate the lessons of this book. We need church leaders for whom the cross of Christ looms large, who delight in God's generosity and so abandon self-service as God's kindness overflows in their lives. Then the world will see Christian integrity. Then the world will see that the living God is both cheerful and delightful to know.

Here, then, in this book is a chance to grow in true magnanimity. It may be a small book, but it is profound. It offers no superficial quick fix, but something far sweeter: a greatness of heart. Read, be cheered, and be enlarged!

Michael Reeves

President and Professor of Theology, Union School of Theology

Foreword
by Daryl Heald

How long does it take for our hearts to be transformed in generosity? This is the question I was laboring with as the world went into lockdown because of Covid restrictions. At Generosity Path our ability to gather and reflect on biblical generosity through 'Journey of Generosity' retreats was almost eliminated. While relaying these concerns to a friend of mine, he challenged me to remember that God is not bound by time when it comes to someone grasping hold of His radical, sacred generosity by choosing to move onto a path of joyful generosity. Can God only transform a heart in 24 hours? Does he need 4 hours? Perhaps just 4 minutes? Over the past year we have learned that transformation is not restricted to timeframes and the ability to gather.

This book from my friend Joel Morris is a gift, reminding us that 'generosity exists because God is triune, and because He is triune, He is happy and He is loving... it is part of His very nature and we are created in His image to be like Him.' Our very DNA was designed by God to express big-hearted, joyful generosity. Joel takes us on a unique journey of scriptural analysis and inspiring stories to help us in our journeys of generosity. This is great news! We don't need to labor for hours to tap into our generosity. It is right there in us at this very moment!

As Christians, we have unique access to this incredible wisdom. Joel elaborates, 'Let's pray and ask God the Father for wisdom to understand and know the Trinity. It is then we can see and know the goodness and overflowing kindness of God. Then we'll be able to glimpse His beauty, greatness, fullness and behold His loveliness.'

He also reminds us of the importance of receiving well. I truly believe this is part of the 'secret sauce' of breaking through to big-hearted generosity. Joel expounds on this concept in his text, encouraging us that if 'you are a good receiver, you will be a rejoicing giver.'

With high esteem, I encourage you to take some time with Joel's thoughtful and loving words. The question he poses is this: 'to whom does God want to overflow through you?' May we all enjoy the profound journey this question provokes in our hearts and lives.

Many blessings,

Daryl Heald
Founder and Board Member, Generosity Path

Preface

If you're thinking, 'oh no, not another book on fundraising!', rest assured, this book isn't that. This book, in my humble opinion, applies to every born again Christian, not just for those who would call themselves donors, philanthropists or givers. It's vitally important for all Christians to rediscover the theology of generosity. I'm biased of course as the author, but just hear me out. I believe this is an area of understanding that we all severely lack in the church today, particularly in the West. The thing is, our understanding and practice of generosity actually says a lot about our knowledge of God and the condition of our own hearts as a result. It says a lot about our hearts. So this is important stuff!

I was moved to write this book in order to drill deeply into the subject of generosity and not to focus on the practical aspects of giving. I observed this deficiency through my work among networks of donors, generosity movements and many church congregations. In the process of writing I recognized a deficiency in myself too. Many books will encourage you to give, tell you that it is a good thing to give and that you'll receive joy when you give. This is true of course, but here, I want to address the 'why?' of giving. For me, this was the burning question no one seemed to be answering. We need more than 'it's a good thing to do'. The motivation to give will determine the kind of giver you'll be, and whether you'll be a happy or reluctant giver. Without addressing this issue, I fear that we are robbing givers of joy and robbing the church of greater kingdom resources. We are also in danger of missing out on God's generous nature and thereby skewing our entire understanding of Him, which has implications upon how we understand His mercy, His love, His anger. We need to see into the very heart of our generous creator God.

I think Christians should be the most cheerfully kind and generous givers. Why should all Christians show profoundly more generosity than non-Christians? (The 'why' is normally always more important than the 'what?') The answer comes down to the motivation, the drive behind the act. Why do people do incredibly generous and selfless acts? Why even be generous at all, let alone being cheerfully generous? The difference between a Christian and a non-Christian is that with a Christian, generosity is overflowing from our life in Christ. It's a heart response because we are recipients of such amazing grace. We didn't save ourselves, we simply said yes to the greatest gift. Logic would then dictate that Christian generosity must stand out from that of the 'normal' worldly generosity. In this sense we Christians should possess an unnatural and godly generosity. A cheerful, outrageous and extravagant generosity. We can be generous in many ways. I'll highlight only a few ways here in order to make application to everyday life, but I think that serving, giving money, giving time and talent, hospitality, food, stuff and good works, can all be bunched together under generosity.

This kind of happy generosity must be driven by love and not merely by pity or our fallen compassion. Although we should feel pity and compassion in giving like Jesus, if we relied on our cold compassion, we would hardly give at all! Neither is generosity motivated by legalistic duty or obligation. It shouldn't be a reluctant generosity, Christians aren't to give grudgingly. If our motivation is to make ourselves feel better, then the motivation is self-centred even though gifts are meant for someone else. Generosity cannot be cheerful because we're in essence trying to buy cheerfulness! Quite often, generosity can actually be transactional. 'Oh, I'll give to that because I like them and I get a free book'. This is quite a common method used in Christian fundraising and I have used it myself in fundraising for my ministry. Ministries feel they must add incentives for people to give. Perhaps the motivation is for tax purposes and it ends up being a legal incentive rather than generosity.

Christian generosity is to be a godly generosity, to be like that of our God. Yes, the unregenerate know how to give good gifts to their children, but how much more our Heavenly Father who gives good gifts to His children! So, we who are His children share this characteristic with our Father: overflowing, rejoicing generosity! We do to others what we would have them do to us. In fact, the Apostle Paul urges us to outdo each other in doing good to each other. How can any one of us actually live this out on a daily basis? How can we sustain this throughout our lives? It seems unobtainable. Well, it is if we try in our own strength and will.

In Mark's Gospel, chapter 12, when Jesus answered the scribe's greatest commandment question, He said:

> You shall love the Lord your God with all your heart and with all your soul and with all your mind and with all your strength. The second is this: you shall love your neighbor as yourself.

These are the greatest commandments in the Bible, according to Jesus. Why are they the greatest? It's because our good works flow out of loving God, and because we love God we can love others as ourselves and do good works for them. That's the key! This is the overflow of gospel generosity. I know that this is the ministry philosophy used by many successful and healthy churches around the world. It is the roadmap for how we can possibly achieve the kind of profound generosity and good works described here. Firstly, we must love the Lord our God with all that we are, then, and only then can we love others as ourselves. Not through a transaction, what we can get in return, but because we love God unreservedly who has given us all things freely.

The Psalmist in Psalm 119:32 declares:

> I will run in the way of your commandments when you enlarge my heart!

We can keep the Lord's commandments because we have a big heart for Him. We no longer have a selfish, self-centred stony heart. God figuratively gives us a heart of flesh that keeps growing in capacity for loving Him and others. The more we enlarge our knowledge of God, the more we love Him and love others. We become big-hearted.

The sad conversation Jesus had with the rich young man in Mark chapter 10 verse 17, shows that he loved his money and possessions more than the God he said he served. If he had loved God as he should, he would love others, and the overflowing love of God would mean that he would be free to bless others, give all that he had and follow Jesus. Instead, he went away from Jesus sorrowful. Jesus exposed the man's heart to himself, and God wasn't his first love. This is why truly generous giving is a healthy practice for Christians, because it helps us to keep loving God first before our wealth, status and possessions. It helps loosen our dependence on material things and keeps our love pointing in the right direction, to Jesus.

As you read this book, please use the opportunity for self-examination and reflection. Writing this book has profoundly challenged me to question my own heart. Am I generous enough? Are my motivations to give, godly? Lay your heart open before God. Let Him work in your heart as He desires you to be conformed to Jesus. Allow the Holy Spirit to change you to become more and more like our rejoicing, generous, life-giving God. Don't let your possessions prevent you from following Jesus. You won't regret abandoning yourself for Jesus. You will regret looking back and wondering, 'what if I had acted on my convictions? What would have happened if I had obeyed the voice of Jesus?' Don't go away sorrowful.

Ask God to enlarge your heart for Him. To love Him and others more than yourself.

Joel Morris
Lockdown, April 2020

1 Introduction

For the love of money is a root of all kinds of evils
(1 Tim. 6:10).

Why do wealthy western Christians feel under pressure and insecure when it comes to talking and thinking about money? We don't like to talk about money or about giving money, do we? Why is that? The Bible isn't embarrassed to talk about it and neither should we as people of the Bible. According to Forbes, money and possessions are the second most referenced topic in the Bible.[1] Jesus taught on it more than sex, heaven and hell.[2] It is obviously an important issue in the Bible to command such attention. It is clear that money can be dangerous and requires much teaching and consideration, though our hearts are drawn to it and seek to obtain it.

---

1   https://www.forbes.com/sites/sherylnancenash/2012/05/24/is-the-bible-the- ultimate-financial-guide/

2   https://www.desiringgod.org/messages/free-from-money-rich-toward-god

The fact that we don't talk about money or generosity today concerns me deeply. I've heard few pastors preach on it—this is even more concerning! It suggests to me that the reason we don't want to talk about money is because there's a deep heart-problem in our society today. It's also a joy and happiness problem. It is a symptom of a problem so deeply rooted in our western culture that we need to work hard to get those deep roots out! The lies we have been sold by the world say that more wealth and possessions equals greater joy and happiness. This is simply not true. So, if we believe the lies, we won't want to talk about money. We'll want to avoid it and keep our dealings locked away and hidden in the dark.

Sadly, we're missing out on so much.

Hilarious Giving

God wants us to be happy people because He Himself is happy and He loves us. The broad theme of the Bible says that the only way we will be happy is through knowing and loving the God who lovingly made us to love and enjoy Him. The problem is that people search for happiness in countless places other than in enjoying their creator God. Some people don't even want to acknowledge the possibility of His existence.

God wants us to be cheerful givers—people who are happy to give and happy in their giving. I realize that we don't naturally put the two things together! What many will associate with happiness is gaining more stuff and enjoying themselves with their stuff. Pretending to be their own god. Getting and keeping the things desired and longed after, like that thing at the top of their Christmas list. They say, 'If I could just get that house or car, it'll make me so happy'.

Making money and getting things easily lead to idolatry, setting up false gods in the place of God. I'm sure we all know deep down inside it doesn't ever last!

Giving, in and of itself doesn't make us happier people. If this were the case, generosity would be a transaction motivation. We'd give to make ourselves feel happy. The more we give, the happier we'll be. Subconsciously you might think, 'I'm giving to feel good. It's a good thing to do. Aren't I a good person?' Giving is not what satisfies ultimately. Christians are already satisfied before the act of giving. If giving generously was the thing that satisfied and made us happy, then the gospel would be works-based. We can't work our way to heaven, why do we think we can work our way to happiness? This is the kind of trap that people fall into isn't it?

Another trap people fall into is giving to get. If we give generously over here, the universe will somehow reward us. If this is our motivation or comfort to be generous, then again, our generosity is flawed. We can also be cajoled into giving through guilt. Charities can play on our emotions. If you don't give to this most worthy of causes then you are a truly terrible and selfish person. Fundraising campaigns will show us pictures of needy people, pull on our heart strings to try and make us give. Please hear me right, I'm not saying we shouldn't give to needy people. The Bible tells us to give to the poor and needy generously, and to look after the widows and orphans.

My point is this; 'Why should Christians be generous?' We instinctively know that being generous with our possessions or time is a good thing, but why? Our motivations for giving can be guilt-driven or perhaps even wanting to impress others? 'Look how generous and good a person I am'—it can give self-worth. The Pharisees in Jesus' day were very good at this! You might write a cheque for a gospel cause to buy the freedom to do whatever you want with what's left so you don't feel guilty about spending on yourself. Do we give reluctantly to charity, but then joyfully buy that coffee machine we've been coveting?

Wealth most definitely can be a snare, it's so deceptive. Please, let's examine our hearts. When I give, do I give reluctantly? Can I truly call myself a cheerful giver? This is such a massive battle for us sinners. What our hearts love, that's what we treasure and want to hold onto. What can change my heart so I give cheerfully and not reluctantly?

It's a titanic struggle inside all of us. Just like some heavyweight bout between two equally matched competitors. Who will win? Well, I think it depends which one you feed! In the blue corner we have Mr. Reluctant, and in the red corner here's Mr. Cheerful. In some rounds, Mr. Reluctant has the dominance, Mr. Cheerful is smacked down by worries about financial security and comfort. In the later rounds perhaps Mr. Cheerful wins through when giving is done sacrificially and wealth isn't held onto for security. Greater security and comfort are discovered elsewhere through fearing the Lord.

We want to be cheerful in life don't we? The world tells us that to be happy we need to prioritize security for family and retirement, then perhaps think about maybe giving a little, somewhat reluctantly. However, there is a corrosiveness that erodes our hearts when riches are held onto and loved. Of course there is, it takes the place of our Savior Jesus. Money and power does corrupt. It is foolish and naive to think that it won't. There is a happiness in giving it away. How do you become cheerful? God is a cheerful giver and never reluctant. This is a wonderful unchanging truth about our Lord. He is not spiteful. He always wants to bless us abundantly more than we can imagine. You may have an understanding of God's desire to bless you as you are reading this. His desire is greater still. The same is true when you fell into sin; God's heart is for the abundant blessing of His people. That isn't dependent on our righteousness.

God loves a cheerful giver because He Himself is a cheerful giver. As we think of God: we start with God as Father, as the Early Church Fathers concluded in the Nicene Creed. God loves Himself. Though, God's love isn't a self-obsessed love but a giving, outflowing and generous love. God is a Father eternally loving His Son through the fellowship of the Holy Spirit. The Son loves the Father back, revealing Him. Jesus lived this out on earth and taught us to pray to God as our Father. Isn't this an amazing trinitarian truth that, when applied, grows our love for Him? He is the only sort of God we can love. God is Father, He is relational and life-giving.[3] Generosity is at the core of the Christian life and our experience of God. God doesn't give sparingly; He gives us

---

3   Michael Reeves, *The Good God* (Milton Keynes: Paternoster, 2014), p. 4.

abundantly more than we can ask or think. God the Father willingly sent His only beloved Son to pay the price we could never pay. The Son generously gives Himself to those who receive, and God makes His home in us. The gospel is good news about the outgoing loving God, giving generously of Himself for the lost. The Father is willing to risk His only Son for our salvation, what are we willing to risk? Our lives, wealth, and homes?[4] We get cheerful in our giving by giving like God, where His grace has been working in our hearts to abound in generosity to others. This verse below is some challenging teaching from Paul's second letter to the Corinthian church on how people should give to support gospel work.

> Whoever sows sparingly will also reap sparingly, and whoever sows bountifully will also reap bountifully. Each one must give as he has decided in his heart, not reluctantly or under compulsion, for God loves a cheerful giver. And God is able to make all grace abound to you, so that having all sufficiency in all things at all times, you may abound in every good work (2 Cor. 9:6-8).

The early church was risking all, every day, for the cause of Christ. Risking their money and comfort. They were in the practice of denying themselves and giving money away to support the growth of the church and God's poor people. In this passage, Paul is arranging for a collection from the Corinthian church for needy Christians still living in Jerusalem. He lays out the way Christians should give and the reason why we should give generously and cheerfully.

---

4   Joel Morris, *Revolutionary God* (Ross-Shire: Christian Focus Publishing, 2019), p. 52.

'Cheerful' is translated from the Greek word 'hilaros,' which is where we get the English word hilarious from. *Strong's Exhaustive Concordance* defines the usage as joyous, cheerful, not grudging. It describes someone who has already been won over, convinced and ready to act cheerily. It comes from our confession of the gospel of Christ, so it is most certainly a gospel issue. The word is only used in this passage where it described spontaneous non-reluctant giving. Each of us is responsible for how we use that with which we have been entrusted. How we treat people created in God's image is always a result of our theology of God and man. We decide in our hearts what we give, why, and to whom we give, and our hearts are shaped by our grasp of God. It is God who gives us the grace to be able to have increasingly large good works like giving generously. We need supernatural grace from God, it is not in our natural capacity. Verse 11 says that we will be enriched to be generous in every way, not to hold onto it for our own safety and comfort.

It is God who supplies seed to the sower and provides harvest in the fields for us all to live and grow. Paul says that God will multiply what we happily give and it will be like sowing for the gospel. Verse 10 of the same chapter in Corinthians, centres around support for gospel ministry and the reaping there will be for His kingdom. Our reward then will be tangible, but not here and now, it will be realized at some future point in heaven stored up for us. The best kind of return we could ever want, where it is totally secure. We are enriched in grace to be generous in every way. This is an unnatural generosity. There's so much here to digest from verse 10 to 15 of this discourse from Paul. As he says, it isn't only supplying the needs of the saints, but overflowing in our thanksgiving to God—as He has been overflowing to us. Imagine churches abounding in all directions, inwardly, outwardly, in thanksgiving to God. Imagine the impact on communities. The Church should be a gloriously radiant display of the abundant generosity of Christ to this world! In giving to support gospel work we are joining with the sower to cheerfully sow bountifully so that the harvest will be cheerful and bountiful. So, we see generosity is a gospel issue. This is important for us to understand in the connection between giving and partnering in God's mission to the world.

Thornton and Newton

The story of John Thornton and John Newton is a great example of financial generosity enabling the work of the gospel, a symbiotic work and faith to ministry relationship. An amazing collaboration between a Christian businessman and a minister of the gospel. It's how it should look in my opinion: vital gospel ministry underpinned by cheerful generosity, we see many examples down through the ages. Newton was an 18th Century Anglican pastor, writer, hymnist, abolitionist and ally of Wilberforce. As a merchant and then Director of the Bank of England, Thornton was a cheerful giver and patron of the evangelical movement. He overflowed with gospel generosity and his vision lined up with that of Newton's. Newton gave Thornton the opportunity of seeing the fruit of his business work translate into spiritual fruit for the gospel. An unusual friendship blossomed between Thornton and

Newton, they traded hundreds of letters. It wasn't a donor-ministry relationship that we might recognize today. It wasn't a relationship where a ministry leader sends an application by email to a faceless board. They were friends, brother-in-arms, committed to pray for each other and they even confessed sin to each other. Sharing doctrine and a care for the nation, they shared a deep concern for the gospel.[5] Both were all in!

As a fundraiser for the ministry I serve, I love this kind of partnership. It is something I actively look for. Providentially, we enjoy this dynamic with a few of our ministry partners. Sometimes I'm able to spend time with them and their families in their homes and enjoy this discipleship dynamic. It's a beautiful thing. Pastors and ministry leaders don't want patrons who try to control and micromanage, as was prevalent in eighteenth-century England. Then, patrons controlled pulpits and what was preached from them. This is obviously an abuse of power and influence, when patrons are paying for control. It was very different with Thornton and Newton, Newton knew his patron's role and guided him to partner in creative and helpful ways for maximum impact for the kingdom. They had huge trust and respect for each other.

Thornton encouraged Newton in his ministry, even enabling and encouraging his hospitality for the poor and needy. I was particularly struck by Newton's letter to Thornton on February 13th, 1779. He says:

> Though I have not the vanity to dedicate any of my services
> to you in public, yet pleasure as well as gratitude prompt me

5   J. Rinehart, *Gospel Patrons: People Whose Generosity Changed the World* (Reclaimed Publishing, 2nd Edition, 2016), pp. 93-125.

to think of you in private, under the Lord to whose goodness I owe your friendship, as my patron. I should be loathe to take any step of importance without your judgment.[6]

This is a lovely window into the friendship and partnership which helped shape the political and spiritual future of the United Kingdom and had significant impact around the world. Such is the power of Christ's body working well together, resourcing and enabling gospel ministry, bringing revival to the Church. Thornton was a cheerful giver, truly happy in Jesus. He never gave grudgingly or reluctantly. God loved this and blessed a long and fruitful friendship.

Thornton overflowed with the grace and love of God, expressed in cheerful generosity and friendship. So, what of this love of God?

Love of God

The Bible tells us that God is love.[7] It's always been in His divine nature. God the Father's love is free and unchangeable. This is unmerited and undeserved and God's own eternal choice.[8] God loved us first and He generously overflows His life and love to us through His only beloved Son Jesus. Our response to this truth isn't a lukewarm and half-hearted love back to Him. Something is drastically wrong with our theology if this is where we are at! The only response we can have back to the Father, if we see, understand and believe, is wholehearted and

---

6   Ibid, p. 108.

7   John 3:16.

8   R.C. Sproul, *Truths We Confess* (Orlando: Reformation Trust Publishing, Revised Edition, 2019), p. 382.

deep love to God our Savior with heartfelt thanksgiving. God is the lover of our souls, forever. We grow to become like Him, overflowing with love to others, to be like unto our loving God, flowing outward with the love that we receive from Him. We aren't to store it up for ourselves and hold onto it. It would seem unloving to be like this, not comprehending the love of God to us. Rather, we are compelled by His rich love to also love others. God always shows us this love.[9] It isn't a hidden love that is merely in word only.

> But God, being rich in mercy, because of the great love with which he loved us, even when we were dead in our trespasses, made us alive together with Christ—by grace you have been saved—and raised us up with him and seated us with him in the heavenly places in Christ Jesus, so that in the coming ages he might show the immeasurable riches of his grace in kindness towards us in Christ Jesus (Eph. 2: 4-7).

Even when we are enemies with God, He loves us and overflows with profound generosity to us. He is a God who foreknew us and as R.C. Sproul says, in his book *Truths We Confess*, God foreloved us. Those whom He foreloved, He also predestined. This is a love that is rock-solid, forever. A love that will not let us go.[10] It's an eternal love that belongs to the Trinity. For God to be eternally loving, He must be more than one. Love is something that one person has for another person, according to C.S. Lewis in his book, *Mere Christianity*.[11] He

---

9   2 Chronicles 5:13.

10   Sproul, p. 382.

11   C.S. Lewis, *Mere Christianity*, (London: Geoffrey Bles, Revised and amplified edition, 3rd Impression, 1961), p. 174.

is love because He is triune. And love only can exist between persons.[12]

In love, God the Son comes to suffer with us. He suffers because He is God and He is love. He enters His creation to become acquainted with suffering and grief. In love, God comes to bear our griefs and carry our sorrows.[13] Yet it was the will of the Father to crush His beloved Son, through love, to save His foreloved whom He predestined. This is love. Love that is willing to suffer and sacrifice for the beloved. God's overflowing love is outflowing to us through the Lord Jesus. We are recipients of grace, righteousness, love, life and gifts from our kind Father. It pleases the Father to give to us in this life, but also in heavenly places where He is. God says we will receive an inheritance, glorious and unfading.[14] He gives us a place with His Son to be beloved. We will share in praise, glory and honor when Christ is revealed. God's goodness to His beloved goes on forever!

Christ will be revealed, and though we haven't seen Him yet, we respond in faith, hope and love for God. We see with the eyes of faith. We praise Him with joy filled with glory because we know and experience His love. The status of 'beloved' is not merely a title that you are awarded. You begin to feel and know the love of God in your heart and life, to such an extent at times you will weep because of His goodness and inexpressible joy. The problem is, God is so profoundly

---

12   R. Letham, *The Holy Trinity* (New Jersey: P&R Publishing, Revised and Expanded Version, 2019), p. 553.

13   Isaiah 53:3-4.

14   1 Peter 1:7.

generous, we sinners struggle to accept it. Perhaps we're not prepared to receive all of God's generosity and as a result we aren't generous to others. What might happen in us if we are open to being filled with power from God? Open to be filled with all the fullness of God. Isn't that a strange thing? We say, 'I'll receive the salvation bit, Lord, but just stop there. I don't want all the other amazing stuff you have for me'.

The Bible says, we have been born again to a living hope. We become beloved children with a wonderful inheritance kept for us in heaven. We don't get downloaded with the full Christian package when we get saved. His power needs to work in us, in spiritual ways. We seldom ask or seek that, we like to be comfortable and safe. In Ephesians 3:18-19, Paul prays that the Church:

> May have strength to comprehend with all the saints what is the breadth and length and height and depth, and to know the love of Christ that surpasses knowledge, that you may be filled with all the fullness of God.

Paul's need to pray this shows that they weren't filled with all the fullness at that time, but God is ready to do abundantly more than we can possibly ask or think.

If we haven't known or experienced the cheerful generosity of God, we're not aware of the possibility of the one who gave everything for us. But, when we see and receive His amazing generosity, of course we realize how generous God is to us. We can still look at ourselves through a negative lens of weakness and failure, overcome with present reality in struggles with sin. Don't forget your present inheritance as a child of God the Father for all eternity, and don't forget you are seated with the Son. Our generous inheritance is that of a son of God. We have to get used to what God has made us to be and who God will make us for all eternity. When we experience God's loving generosity, we will also be generous because we know and experience His overflowing love.

2 Overflowing God

Every good gift and every perfect gift is from above, coming down from the Father of lights, with whom there is no variation or shadow due to change (James 1:17).

The theology of generosity is completely trinitarian: generosity exists because God is triune, and because He is triune, He is happy and He is loving. So, generosity is a consequence of the divine nature of God. What is the divine nature of God? God loves Himself and is generous to Himself and to His creation. He is three, distinct, coequal persons, so He is not being self-centred in loving Himself. God the Father is the generously overflowing source: eternally generating the Son and they, in turn, are 'spirating' or breathing out the Holy Spirit, and the Spirit is poured out on the Church. So, the triune God is active and outgoing. When we explore the nature of God, we see that generosity is an important subject to Him. It is part of His very nature and we are created in His image to be like Him. We are designed to be in community.

Athanasius, the Bishop of Alexandria in Egypt in the 4th Century, taught that the Son, who is the Word of God, brings us the grace and love of the Father, who in the beginning had made all things out of nothing. The Athanasian Creed states, the Son is eternally generated by the Father, so the Father cheerfully sends out the Son in salvation, giving eternal life. He pours out the Holy Spirit at Pentecost, sealing our salvation. This 4th Century Bishop knew that God is the happy fount of living water we are to drink from. We see the generous nature of God reflected in creation all around us.

> The Father was neither made nor created nor begotten from anyone. The Son was neither made nor created; he was begotten from the Father alone. The Holy Spirit was neither made nor created nor begotten; he proceeds from the Father and the Son (Athanasian Creed).[1]

Our Good God

Life and love continually overflow from Him to His creation. All good things come from Him, the author and creator of life, because God is good. Why is this important? When Christians serve others or give a gift to help someone, it points people to their good, overflowing, creator God. Good works don't replace the gospel though, we never stop telling people the good news about Jesus. Why would we bless people with material help while depriving them of the one thing that can

---

1   E. Gibson, *The Three Creeds* (The Oxford Library of Practical Theology, 1909), p. 216.

save their very soul from eternal judgment without God? No, the gospel is the ultimate generosity from the ultimate giver.

God the Father is eternally loving the Son in the fellowship of the Spirit, He is a Father to His Son eternally. That's why He is love, because He is eternally triune and why we can trust Him and experience His love too. God generously, sacrificially, gives of Himself to us by sending His Son to save us and bring us into that same loving fellowship. The Trinity makes salvation possible and sweet. 1 John 4:7 says:

> Anyone who does not love does not know God, because God is love.

The beloved should at the very least love one another in the fellowship of the Spirit. But, we are to go further than this and love our neighbor as we love ourselves. You may say, 'I just can't do that, it's too much!' Dear friend, we have been given the Spirit of adoption, so we share what the Son shares with the Father. So, we can be gracious and overflowing with love to our neighbor. If we are adopted and become children of God, knowing and experiencing the love of God, then we simply must love others. True love is self-giving and sacrificial.

God shows us His love by sending His Son whom He loved, to be the payment for our sin. Imagine what it cost God to pay our debts. We have been redeemed by the precious blood of God's Son. What Father could offer such a sacrifice? Yet, this is what Fathers and Mothers did during the World Wars. Many supported their children going away to fight a war in another part of the world, perhaps never to return. Being a parent means to love, to give our lives to beget children. So, the pain of sending sons to go and die for others is such a high price. God is able to pay such a high price out of His fullness. He is out-flowing His fullness to us through the Son and the Spirit. We who are gathered in the Son are growing up in every way into Him.[2]

Religion doesn't come near this, because salvation is adoption into a family, you can't buy or work your way in. It has to be free, it has to be a gift. It's being brought into a loving relationship with the Father through Jesus. The eternal life of sonship in the Son of God is including us in His life. How good and generous is our God? The Father loving the Son and the Son loving the Father in the fellowship of the Spirit. Nothing makes us more godly than us loving the Father and the Son as the Spirit enables us. This eternal Fatherhood means that God the Father has no Father Himself, and the Son, eternally generated by the Father, has no beginning. This is indeed a mystery. It is too wonderful for human comprehension.

> If any of you lacks wisdom, let him ask God, who gives generously to all without reproach, and it will be given him (James 1:5).

We need precious wisdom from God to help us understand deep mysteries. Wisdom is that which the Bible tells us can bring us to God and so to fear Him. When we understand more of God and who He is, we feel the weightiness of His glory, we deepen our love for Him. James tells us that we need wisdom to be steadfast under trials. Wisdom is a gift that does not corrupt like riches and power. Wisdom is a gift to

2   Ephesians 4:15.

the humble. It is given as a good example for us to follow as we ask God for spiritual gifts. God is cheerfully generous and gives without reproach. So, we His children should not shy away from asking our Father for gifts to help us to be steadfast Christians. Not gifts of prosperity or comfort, but gifts that will help build us up in love.

Let's pray and ask God the Father for wisdom to understand and know the Trinity. It is then we can see and know the goodness and overflowing kindness of God. Then we'll be able to glimpse His beauty, greatness, fullness and behold His loveliness. Wisdom enabling our hearts to be won to God and grow in love for Him over the things of the world. This is the way to prepare for any trial. Then we will be like the Son who went through the fire and great suffering, giving His all gladly. Death could not hold Him because the Father is eternally begetting Him. The whole Godhead is working to overthrow the curse and bring forth a new creation.

His Generous Creation

The whole of creation is a grand exhibit of the Father's generosity. R.C. Sproul describes the classic Christian doctrine of creation—out of nothing (*ex nihilo*), in his book *Truths We Confess*.[3] God spoke the universe into being from absolutely nothing. From absolute zero—not even one atom—to the incredible planet and star-filled glorious universe, with the most imaginative and diverse life to occupy our world. There was nothing preexisting that could be adapted and reformed

---

3   R.C. Sproul, pp. 100-102.

into this world. God isn't like us in that all we can do is take existing stuff and make other stuff from it.

I'm reminded of a friend who is a highly regarded wildlife artist. He doesn't create beautiful works of art from nothing. There is the canvas and the paints, and there is the inspiration for his art. He needs to go out on field trips to see and capture inspiration for the canvas. He needs material to work from to interpret into amazing and beautiful creations of art which people will pay to adorn their walls. This creativity makes use of materials that are readily available, but only God can create something out of nothing. We depend on all God has made for us and we depend on Him every second for our very existence.[4] Isn't God so kind and good? Now we see that life itself is actively and originally overflowing from God.

We've said earlier that generosity is a consequence of God's divine nature and that the Father is the generously overflowing source, like a river. We see that He is generously generating a creation, and cheerfully delighting in all of it as it reflects His goodness and glory. Little wonder then that creation itself reveals our generous creator God.[5] Here's a glimpse into the new creation from the book of Revelation.

> Then the angel showed me the river of the water of life, bright as crystal, flowing from the throne of God and of the Lamb through the middle of the street of the city; also, on either side of the river, the tree of life with its twelve kinds

---

4   Ibid, p. 103.

5   Robert Letham, *Systematic Theology* (Wheaton, Illinois: Crossway, 2019), pp. 282-283.

of fruit, yielding its fruit each month. The leaves of the tree were for the healing of the nations (Rev. 22:1-2).

In Revelation 22, verse 1, the Apostle John gets shown the new creation in its full glory displayed with the city of God and Jesus at its center, shining, outflowing with light and life from the Father—He is the radiance of the Father's glory. Glory and love radiate outwards, teaching us again of a God who doesn't need to receive but give out. And in the new creation is the city called the New Jerusalem with the river of the water of life springing up, gushing from the throne of God and Jesus. The river brings life and fruitfulness in full abundance. What a powerful image of rejoicing generosity! The water of life, happily bubbling and gushing out of the throne of God. Doesn't this make the heart glad?

Jonathan Edwards, describes it as,

> The Son of God, who is the brightness of the Father's glory, appears there in the fullness of his glory, without that garb of outward meanness in which he appeared in this world. The Holy Ghost shall there be poured forth with perfect richness and sweetness, as a pure river of the water of life, clear as crystal, proceeding out of the throne of God and of the Lamb.[6]

This river of living waters theme is a helpful illustration for us when we think about generosity and the heart of God. John 4 shows the Father sending His Son to bring living water to the thirsty. The Bible says, whoever drinks of the water He gives,

---

6   Jonathan Edwards, *Charity and Its Fruits* (Edinburgh: Banner of Truth, 1969), p. 330.

shall never thirst again. The water Jesus gives will become in the drinker, a spring of water welling up to eternal life. In John chapter 7, Jesus says that the living water is the Spirit. So the Father sends the Son to send the Spirit! The Holy Spirit is being poured out in our hearts, a fountain of eternal life just like we see in the book of Revelation. All springs flowing together like a big river. I love that image of God as a river, overflowing from heaven to earth through His body, the Church.[7] You too will overflow with the Holy Spirit, with abundant spiritual fruit: love, joy, peace, patience, kindness, goodness, faithfulness, gentleness and self-control.[8] This is the abundant life, God's people bring abundance of life and love to the world around them like a fountain. Giving out, not grabbing and holding. We drink in Christ and receive the Spirit, then overflow with as much as we receive from God.

If we go back to the Old Testament, Ezekiel chapter 47 describes Ezekiel's vision of the river of life flowing from out of the sanctuary of the temple—this looks prophetically forward to the book of Revelation. It looks past the restoration of Jerusalem after the exile to Babylon, to a better Jerusalem prophesied in Revelation 22. In Ezekiel's vision, as in Revelation, the river of life is flowing out from under the temple—the temple is symbolic for the Christ who would be killed and then resurrected after three days. Ezekiel's river flows east from the mercy seat, from under the temple into the dead sea, making it fresh once again and bringing life to it.

---

7   Joel Morris, *Revolutionary God*, pp. 69-70.

8   Galatians 5: 22-23.

There is a river of love, providentially flowing from creation's Eden through history and on into the new creation and forever. It never stops flowing, because God the Father is generously overflowing through the Son and we are in Him, and He is in God. We should have a similar life-bringing impact in our communities, as rivers, cheerfully overflowing from Christ our source. Our love and cheerful generosity can bring life to what once was cold and dead. What beautiful, active, union, when the Son of God's bride overflows with love to the world to reflect God's glory.

The Providence of God

When I think of God's generosity, I also think of His providence. We can also consider God's divine providence as a river. Constant, flowing, unceasing, upholding, sustaining life and bringing fruitfulness. The word providence comes from the Latin root to see beforehand, what is needed. For the Christian, providence means God's faultless care of the world and His sovereign governance, direction and upholding. Providence is the continued action of God beginning with creation. God can't help but be cheerfully generous to His creation. He does really have the whole world in His hands! The Lord provides for the world, for all people, but He also provides for His people, and takes special care of His Church, bringing all good things for her good.[9] Could you consider your timely gift a wonderful providence from the Lord for some needy soul?

---

9   Westminster Confession of Faith, 5, Of Providence.

God's providence is His outflowing generosity working through His foresight. His work of salvation is a good example of this. God both sees and knows the need, He takes steps by sending His only Son to be the sacrifice for us. The Lord provides for our every need. God's providence is introduced to us in Genesis 22:14:

> So Abraham called the name of that place, 'The Lord will provide'; as it is said to this day, 'On the mount of the Lord it shall be provided.'

Abraham refers to God as LORD Jireh, meaning The Lord will provide.[10] Abraham adds this attribution to God's very name to describe Him. By faith, when he built the altar Abraham knew the Lord had a plan and a purpose, and he knew God would provide a sacrifice that would please Him. Abraham was willing to sacrifice his only God-promised son and not withhold him from God. So, God stopped Abraham from plunging the knife in and provided a substitutionary sacrifice. Of course, this is a massive prophetic signpost pointing to Christ on the cross, our lamb of God. Like Abraham, God was willing not to withhold His only Son to be the lamb offering for our sin. Even back in Genesis, God is preaching the gospel. He is teaching us a vital truth, that He and only He has the ability to truly provide (it is easy to lose sight of this if you live in the West). It is *just-in-time* provision, as He knows in advance what we need and when we need it. God is absolutely trustworthy, having planned our future, He also resources

---

10   R.C. Sproul, p. 125.

what we need and when, to meet us in our need as we walk with Him.

At the beginning of the great global lockdown of 2020, the first thing people did all over the world was to rush out and stock up on essential supplies. It was interesting to see toilet paper as initially the most sought-after item. Fathers and mothers had the foresight and were making sure they could provide for their families should these items become scarce.

God does this on a much larger scale of course, and He isn't driven by fear to give us things we don't really need.

A great example of God's provision for His people is found in the book of Joshua, chapter 24. Joshua gathers all the people together at Israel's capital city of the time—Shechem. God speaks to the people through Joshua, retelling the story of their nation from His perspective:

> Long ago, your fathers lived beyond the Euphrates, Terah, the father of Abraham and of Nahor; and they served other gods. Then I took your father Abraham from beyond the River and led him through all the land of Canaan, and made his offspring many. I gave him Isaac. And to Isaac I gave Jacob and Esau. And I gave Esau the hill country of Seir to possess, but Jacob and his children went down to Egypt (Josh. 24:2-4).

This is a remarkable list of God's overflowing goodness and generosity to His covenant people. It's a list of His faithful provision for them, God's special providence for His people, following His direction. It began before they even knew Him. He took Abraham, led him, gave him an heir and multiplied his children into a nation. He gave land to live on, He protected, He plagued their enemies, He fought for them, led and fed them. The land He gave to them came ready to live on with ready-made cities, vineyards and orchards. It was all of God and not by their own strength and might. God the provider gave everything to Israel.

How can God give away land that belongs to the people who lived there? It all belongs to God, His land to give, and why not have people living on your land who you've nurtured and who worship you? God's generosity flows to His people through the fruit of the land, even when they weren't honoring Him. This is such undeserved, gracious generosity from a loving and merciful God. The people were instructed to give back to God from the land, tithes (a tenth) were gathered from the producing land and distributed locally to support the tribe of priests and support the poor. Both groups of people had no lands as inheritance.

A tithe can be a helpful guide for people to begin to practice giving, but it seems to me something relating to the covenant and the land. For those of us who are not Jewish landowners, I'm not sure the concept can be neatly cut and pasted into our context. If we are giving our tithes out of legalism or duty, then we aren't being cheerfully generous, we are merely following 'the law'. Is there any sacrifice involved on our part? This is helpful for all of us to reflect on. There are quite a few occurrences throughout the Old Testament of a freewill offering from the people to God.

One of these is found in 1 Chronicles 29, at the end of David's reign, as he prepares for a large development project with his people. God has appointed Solomon, David's son, to oversee the building of the temple, but David has done a lot of the preparation work. He has sourced a lot of the materials ready for the work to begin. As a person of extremely high net worth, he has also pledged his own precious metals and gems to the project under the stewardship of a faithful man. This is a freewill offering, not a tithe. Then David invites the people to join him in rejoicing generosity to the Lord. And they do! This is biblical matched funding. The people respond with overflowing, joyous generosity, matching David's giving and they enjoyed giving with a whole heart. Meaning, they are cheerfully giving all, freely, with joy to the Lord. This isn't a hesitant generosity. King David responds with great rejoicing, because the people enter into his joy with him.

David then responds with prayer, blessing the Lord with the assembly of the people. He declares that God is blessed, He is a forever happy God. David says that all of creation belongs to God, all the riches, power and the glory. All that they have given freely, belongs to God anyway. So, what does giving freely mean? I take it to mean they are giving cheerfully and without holding back. God sees the heart of the giver, and judges the motive and the gift. It must be sacrificial if they're not holding back. There isn't any ulterior motive, but hearts that are directed to God. This is an upright motive and is pleasing to the Lord, because it is after God's own overflowing heart. The king and his people are giving like their God. This speaks something of our union through generosity as an expression of worship. This cheerful generosity must be a constant heart posture for the Christian, as having a heart after God's own heart. This is what David prayed for his own son to have, a heart that would give, humbly, freely and joyously. Wholly for God. A heart after God's own heart.

Overflowing generosity, us giving back to the Lord a portion of what we have been blessed with, is right. Not as a payment, but in the spirit of the tithe and the freewill offering of praise. Generosity forms part of our worship to God, our reasonable service. As we give to bless those in need, those in ministry, we are giving back to God what already belongs to Him. David's desire was that the people build the greatest house for God, with all the riches poured into it. That first temple was a shadow of the true temple, the true dwelling place of God—the Church. How could we not pour our all into its building? Brick by brick and person by person.

Back in 1 Chronicles chapter 18, David talks about his victories and the expansion of his kingdom. God had just made an amazing covenant with him in chapter 17, and instead of allowing David to build God a house, God says that He's going to build David's house.

Ultimately, prophesying of the coming of the son of David, the King of Kings, Jesus. This opens up an amazing heart response from David as he sits before the Lord. Chapter 18 talks about the various battles David fought, and spoils of war he plundered from the likes of the Philistines and the Syrians. He shows generosity with others and as we know, dedicated the gold, silver and bronze to the Lord's work. In all his successes and accumulated wealth, David gave back to the Lord in thankfulness for His providence and blessing. He didn't see wealth as belonging to him, but to God.

What do we learn as rejoicing givers from God's gracious providence? We know we should grow to be like God. To be like David, a man after God's own heart. Okay, we will never have the foresight God has, but we can be informed, planned and strategic in our giving, being clear in direction and vision. It is good to be giving with our head as well as our heart. Now, I realize that people tend to have a lot of fear about giving money away. This is quite a big obstacle to generosity. People think, 'If I give to this cause or to my church, will I be left with enough?' I'm convinced we know deep down that this can't be right. We give from what God has given us and trust He will continue to provide for us. We don't hold onto resources just in case God fails to provide. We give generously, knowing and trusting God has already taken steps to provide for us in the future. What we give away is part of God's providence for others. This is also important for pastors, church leaders and ministry leaders to understand and trust in God's provision.

George Müller (19th Century)

George Müller was a man who knew the provision of the Lord almost on a daily basis. He was one of the founders of the Plymouth Brethren movement, a pastor, preacher, missionary and the Director of the Ashley Down orphanage in Bristol, England. Amazingly, he cared for over 10,000 orphans in his lifetime and established many schools to provide education to hundreds of thousands. At the age of seventy, he traveled to forty-two countries and preached to over three million people.[11]

As Müller began his ministry to orphans in 1832, he followed in the footsteps of a Lutheran clergyman, August H. Franke of Halle, Germany. Müller studied theology in Halle and ended up staying at Franke's orphanage for two months. As George started out, he read the biography of Franke who founded the Orphan Houses of Halle. At the time, Franke had built the largest charity for poor children in the world, housing, clothing, feeding and teaching the children. Müller read of how Franke trusted God would provide for his endeavor and how God supplied abundantly. We see throughout history how when the Lord prepares someone for a work of service, there are many helpful examples to follow down a well-beaten path.[12]

Such a ministry as caring for orphans, something so near to the heart of Christ. With no other way of funding the initiative but by relying on the generosity of others he trusted the Father's faithful provision to provide everything for those poor souls in such poverty.

Imagine how heavy the burden might be of all those hungry mouths to feed, buildings to care for, staff to support, clothes to buy etc. Without even asking for a penny from anyone, the Lord was faithful and provided what was needed with increasing supply, year after year. This was the Müller funding model. It was always just enough! According to the need,

---

11   www.mullers.org

12   A.T. Pierson, *George Müller of Bristol*, (London: James Nisbet & Co. 1900, 3rd Edition) p. 103.

the right provision arrived in time. The prayers were many, as were the needs, but the cheerful provider did not let George down. The burden was not George's but God's, and for God to fail to supply the need and for the children to starve was inconceivable to George. He said, 'the Lord thus impressed on me from the beginning that the orphan houses and work were His, not mine.'[13]

George gratefully received showers and rivers of blessing from the Lord, ample donations given by those with abundance of riches as well as those with abundance of poverty. Yes, cheerful generosity isn't only for the wealthy but also for the poor. Why rob the poor of such joy? Müller experienced joy too as the receiver. Not only in seeing prayers answered, but he'd be refreshed through participating in cheerful, though often costly, gifts with the givers. He breathed in the sweet scent of these sacrifices rising to heaven.

One of the first to give to support the ministry was a very poor needlewoman who brought one hundred pounds (a very large sum at the time). This is an incredible sacrifice made by someone who endured many hardships including long hours of work and inadequate accommodation. On average, she earned three shillings and sixpence (just over ten British pounds in today's money). She herself was destitute. So how did she come by such an amount? It would have been equivalent to just over six thousand pounds today. It had come to her from her grandmother's estate as a legacy. George even tried to talk her out of it, not wanting to be too hasty to grasp

---

13   Ibid, p. 325.

at any gift whatever the need. He wanted to make sure she was giving with the right motivation, that she had counted the cost. She had come to her decision sober-minded and calmly, reasoning that if the Lord had spilled His last drop of blood for her, how could she not give Him one hundred pounds?[14]

Müller's mite-giving widow became a loyal supporter and recurring donor. This humble needlewoman helped seed the ministry for orphans in Bristol. She was known to have given food and clothing in secret, gifts that were disproportionate to her means. She wasn't tithing, nor blowing a trumpet to draw attention to herself. She worked hard to make money so she could joyfully give to help the poor. She lived a life of overflowing generosity, in the end all her money gone. Too frail to work, her overflowing God didn't leave her destitute.[15] Faithfully in prayer appealing to God, she never suffered any lack. She didn't worry that if she gave away the one hundred pounds she would not have enough for herself later. She didn't think, 'what if I need it when I can no longer work?'. No pension for her either! This is extraordinarily beautiful faith. Even though she was suffering in the end in her body, her mouth was continually filled with praises for her God. Christ was before her to welcome her to her inheritance kept in heaven with Him. She'd not earned her way to heaven, she'd received by grace, free salvation paid for by Christ's life, given on the cross.

---

14   Ibid, p. 326.

15   Ibid, p. 327.

3 The Greatest Gift

For God so loved the world, that he gave his only Son, that whoever believes in him should not perish but have eternal life (John 3:16).

God is overflowing with love. There's no greater example of God's love in all of history than when He redeemed people back to Himself through His Son on the cross. God sends His Son to the world to live a perfect life without sin. Then, outside the city, He sends Him to the place of death, to willingly be the sacrificial lamb to take our place. This is the most incredible truth! God who is overflowing with life and love, even giving out His very life with cheerful generosity. God, the greatest donor, proves His love and generosity to us by bleeding for us on the cross.

You might be thinking that this is all very theoretical. How can I actually experience God's generosity in my life? How can I know and feel the love of God and His grace pouring into my life? The Bible tells us the answer. All we have to do to receive

God's free gift is trust in Jesus and what He has accomplished for us on the cross. We can be recipients and partakers of His grace. Jesus isn't a reluctant Savior, He delights to show us mercy. He's a cheerful giver, giving His all as a man and God. All sufficient for us poor sinners, He is enough for your life. Through the cross we see that at God's core He is an abundant giver, overflowing with generosity.

> *There is a fountain filled with blood*
> *Drawn from Immanuel's veins;*
> *And sinners plunged beneath that flood,*
> *Lose all their guilty stains.*
>
> *The dying thief rejoiced to see*
> *That fountain in his day;*
> *And there have I, as vile as he,*
> *Washed all my sins away.*[1]

At the Cross

It's a scene perhaps many of us have imagined in our mind's eye. Jesus hanging on the cross. Perhaps you've watched a movie about the life of Jesus and the crucifixion. His precious blood running down His torn body, soaking into the splintery rough wood and spilling onto the dusty ground, His heart thumping through His chest. Giving His blood, His life and His all, to save us. To make a way of salvation for all people who simply believe in Him. The Lamb of God, taking away the sin of the world. Why did He do it? Why go through hell for those who didn't know or love Him. Why would a God

---

1   From the hymn 'There is a fountain filled with blood' by William Cowper, 1771.

who knew absolute power and glory, humble Himself to allow His creation to cause Him such grief and suffering?

In his book, *The Pleasures of God*, John Piper makes the point that it pleased God to bruise His Son and bring Him to grief to resolve the dissonance between His love for His glory and His love for sinners. God wanted to show us sinners mercy, to heal and save us, but He also loves His glory. He writes:

> Something needed to be done to save sinners, and at the same time magnify the worth of His glory. God lays our sin on Jesus and abandons Him to the shame and slaughter of the cross.[2]

Piper makes the important point that everything Jesus did in life and death He did for the glory of His Father. Jesus glorified the Father on the cross and brings God's love for sinners in harmony with His love for His glory. God's generosity is always tied to His glory, and ours should be too. God had passed over the former sins of Old Testament saints. What? Yes, God was willing to bring His righteousness into question because He loved sinners. So, the Father put the Son forward as a propitiation by His blood (Rom. 3:25), appeasing His wrath on sin. Jesus makes it right by becoming the payment, once for all, proving God's righteousness and magnifying His glory on the cross. These are the highest stakes.

Our works have never been enough to save us, even since the beginning. Those saints in the Old Testament, before

---

2   John Piper, *The Pleasures of God* (Ross-Shire: Mentor, 2006), pp. 161-165.

Christ, trusted in what the laws and ceremonies signified— salvation through the coming Redeemer.[3] The Bible says, 'For all have sinned and fall short of the glory of God' without exception. Only Jesus' perfect, precious sacrifice was enough to save. That's why the Father sent His Son to give His life for us all. We can only be justified by this free gift and by this divine transaction, we are redeemed back to God through the work of the Son. We can come to Jesus and rest in His righteousness because Christ infinitely fulfilled the righteous requirement of the law. Jesus obeyed His Father to the full and without hesitation because of His love for sinners and love of the glory of the Father. He came to fill what we lack with His all-sufficient righteousness. It is apparent that Jesus' mission had two goals: saving sinners and saving the worth of the Father's glory. Is your generosity tied to God's glory?

So you see, salvation is a complete work of the Trinity, overflowing with divine, eternal love for the world. Jesus gave His body over to be broken, shamed and tortured. He is Isaac's substitute, laying Himself down on the altar as a sacrifice to take Abraham's knife. He gave His very lifeblood on the cross so that God's justice would pass over us. More hurtful than the physical pain and suffering, the Son of God was made sin for us.

> For our sake he made him to be sin who knew no sin, so that in him we might become the righteousness of God (2 Cor. 5:21).

---

3   R.C. Sproul, p. 186.

The God who loves His Son and His glory passionately, made His Son to be sin, so we could become righteous. This is something that can go over our heads. We wrestle with the reality of what this Bible verse means. God the Son gave His life, became sin for me. Jesus became a High Priest, offering Himself as a sacrificial lamb of God for His elect throughout history. He gave everything so that we could become like Him as adopted children. The only righteousness in the universe is God's, and in Jesus that's what we become through our union with Him. Jesus did it all for us so we could receive the greatest gift completely free. Look just how generous our God is.

Let this sink in to your heart. This incredible loving generosity flows through the cross from the heart of the triune God. It doesn't stop there, as if that wasn't enough. As His blood-bought children, we become more and more like Jesus, and have the full status of sonship with the Father. We become like the Son, especially in how we love. We love and delight in God, therefore we can love others. The love of Christ compels us to be cheerfully generous, like Him. It's a gospel generosity, overflowing from the cross backwards as well as forwards. This is the absolutely scandalous generosity of God. People living in the Old Testament were saved as much by the work of Jesus on the cross as we are living in A.D. We are saved in the same way as Abraham. The only difference is that he trusted in the promises of God that hadn't yet been fulfilled. What a vantage point we have living under the new covenant.[4]

---

4   Ibid, pp. 184-185.

Our motivation for good works must flow out of the gospel and our faith in Jesus. If not, we can fall into the trap of trying to work our way into God's good graces rather than enjoying His grace. That's never going to work! We can try to save people through our good works rather than through the message of the gospel. We need our good works to flow out of our love of Christ and the gospel. They flow naturally from God's abundance and grace welling up in us. As we grow in Christ, so does our love for others.

God's overflowing generosity is such that He provides salvation completely. He clothes us in rich righteousness, adopts us as highly valued sons, He fills us with grace, love, life and His Spirit. He gives us peace from heaven. All of this is a voluntary, free, grace gift. He does all the work, all we need to do is accept and believe. We don't need to be born into nobility or have wealth to pay for any of this. Actually, riches make it more difficult to get hold of this!

Revolutionary Force

Can you imagine what this means for someone who has nothing? Wearing years old rags, sleeping rough on the streets, smelly and undesirable, no hope and no prospects in life. Can you see what godly, overflowing generosity can do in our world? How revolutionary and earth-shattering a force it is. Imagine what we could do if we practiced what we have received from God? The difference it can make in people's lives and the power of preaching Christ with cheerful gospel generosity. We overflow because of the gospel, so we mustn't forget the gospel in our giving. We have received such generosity and we want others to receive the ultimate generosity. Just like God the Father gifted His only beloved Son to Mary and Joseph to be born in a lowly stable.

King Jesus wasn't born into a palace with riches or a title. He was born into a very lowly situation. He came from the highest of heights into a borrowed cattle feed trough, born into a poor working-class family. Mary and Joseph needed to rely on the generosity of the innkeeper, the innkeeper did the best he could for the poor couple in need. Generosity is intrinsically part of the birth of Jesus. Cheerful generosity is also tied to the story of Jesus' death and resurrection: Joseph of Arimathea gave his own tomb for the use of Jesus. I love the symmetry here. It reminds me that Jesus relied on the Father's provision through the generosity of others, for their joy.

How can we be practically generous in the way God is? We can be generous with money and time, hospitality and possessions, but not necessarily in a Christlike way. Every Christian growing more like Christ exhibits His attributes. Servant-hearted, merciful, generous, compassionate. It's an overflow of the love and grace of God, via Jesus, through us by the Spirit. We might be moved to give more than is comfortable, how can we do that? Is it our own piety that moves us to make such personal sacrifices or is it something from outside of ourselves?

We know from chapter one of Paul's second letter to the Corinthians that it is God Himself who establishes us all together in Christ and has anointed us by His Spirit. We must therefore willingly submit ourselves to the work of the Holy Spirit in our hearts, as we are gradually being beautified and established in Jesus. On top of paying for our sins on the cross, taking our sins on Himself and imputing His own righteousness to us, God also gives us a down payment of His Spirit in our hearts. Whoa! How generous is our God?! A guarantee of our salvation, justification, beautification and all the promises of God.

We are recipients of such extravagant generosity. All we have to do is receive the free gift of God. The Spirit is God's guarantee to us that we have really received something. He's so tangible and present in the day-to-day of life, or at least He should be. Something extraordinary, supernatural and absolutely real. A present reality that looks to eternity with surety and confidence. An immovable royal seal that should remind us of the immeasurable riches of our eternal inheritance. Why are we holding onto the stuff we have earned when we have been given so much more? How precious is the stuff, status, and life we have worked for and built for ourselves?

Jesus says that it is actually difficult for rich people to enter heaven. It's not easy or straight forward because of our accumulated riches and possessions. They get in the way. They prevent us seeing Jesus, standing between us and Him. These are things the heart clings to and loves, they make it difficult for us to get in the door! Jesus makes the statement to His followers after He challenged the rich young man in Mark 10:23. He said, 'How difficult it will be for those who have wealth to enter the kingdom of God!' Why was this such a shocking statement for Jesus to come out with? Why were the disciples astonished at this? They asked, 'who then can be saved?' We tend to prioritize people with wealth and status don't we? There are classes in every human society. In Israel, those who had wealth and status had prime place in the temple. Of course, they were considered to be 'in the kingdom', because they seemed worthy of being there. This is a worldly perception and value system. Not so in God's kingdom, it's the complete opposite. Jesus shatters our value of wealth and status.

This rich young man loved his money and possessions more than God. They owned his heart, though he hadn't realized. Jesus looked at him and loved him. He gently shows him his own heart. He loves him even though he hasn't kept the most important commandments.

How deceitful is the love of riches if we allow it room in our hearts. When it came to the crunch, he clung to his wealth, his own comfort and desires. Instead of abandoning all like the simple fishermen and embracing the Son of God, he turned away because he loved his wealth and influence too much. He could have come as he was and Jesus would have accepted him. If he had truly loved God first, with all his heart, he would also have loved others as God loves them. The overflow would mean that he would be free to bless others, give all that he had and follow Jesus with great rejoicing. Instead, he went away from Jesus deeply sorrowful.

This is why truly generous and happy giving is a healthy practice for all Christians especially the wealthy, because it helps us to keep loving God first before our possessions. It helps keep our love pointing in the right direction to Jesus.

And, if one day Jesus tells us to give all away and follow Him, we shall be able!

From this encounter with this rich young ruler, I find it interesting how John Mark then moves us onto an account of Jesus foretelling His death and resurrection on the road to Jerusalem. He points us forward to the moment when Jesus would be poured out as an overflowing love offering to God. Jesus walked the talk. He holds Himself up to His followers as an example to follow, not to store up treasures on earth, but to follow His suffering and servant example. This is the way He invites His disciples on, to gain a treasure house of inheritance in heaven from a life lived in service on earth. Are we willing to follow Jesus through suffering and death, into glory, to be with Him? God calls us to live a life overflowing, to pour out our lives like Jesus. We will reap our sure reward when we reach glory to be with Jesus in eternity.

The Overflow

See that you also excel in this grace of giving (2 Cor. 8:7, NIV)

When Christians sacrifice in giving, it's not from a place of legalism or duty, that just isn't enough. It is, as Paul calls it, an act of grace. For our generosity to be both sacrificial and cheerful, it can only be through the overflow of love for God and people. Legalism or duty isn't prepared to make this kind of sacrifice. We can glean so much from the Macedonian church through this window into first-century financial support for ministry. Paul writes this about them to encourage generosity in others:

In a severe test of affliction, their abundance of joy and their
extreme poverty have overflowed in a wealth of generosity
on their part. For they gave according to their means, as I can
testify, and beyond their means, of their own accord, begging
us earnestly for the favor of taking part in the relief of the
saints (2 Cor. 8:2-4).

Kingdom-minded, overflowing generosity, is being prepared
to give all for the sake of Christ and the gospel, because of love.
An overflow of love of God and His Word, is exceedingly more
powerful than love of the world. The filling of the abundance
of God allows us to give all, even our lives, if that is where God
leads us. So, like Jesus, there is joy instead of reluctance. Paul
doesn't command this but encourages it as a proof of genuine
love. Paul then lifts up the Lord Jesus Christ as an example,
who was rich but became poor. So that through His poverty,
we might become rich.

I remember leading a missionary team in the interior of
Panama in 2003 when I worked with Operation Mobilisation
as a young man. In spite of my youth, the jungle humidity and
heat were crippling, sapping all energy until all you could do
was lay down exhausted. The conditions were debilitating. On
one occasion, I had to go to lead a service in the town center in
a few hours and I simply couldn't get up. I remember thinking
to myself, 'how am I going to do this?' All my duty and good
works couldn't get me up from my bed. Then, I remembered a
book I had been reading by John Piper called *Let the Nations
Be Glad*. I prayed to God to help me, to give me the energy
to preach as an act of worship, as an overflow of my love and
life in Him. I had been wrestling with my idea of being a

missionary and feeling crushed under the weight of the duty I felt. I couldn't do it in my own strength.

Reading Pastor John's book revolutionized my understanding of missionary work and helped liberate me from the weight of responsibility of being a missionary. I suddenly found the strength to go and lift up Jesus with great passion to the town. Duty and your own strength will only get you so far.

We see this when Jesus calls normal people to be fellow servants. They overflow from a full heart of love and the Spirit of God as they work to make disciples in the world. Jesus' followers don't want to keep the blessing for themselves. They want to be blessed by Him and enjoy Him, but disciples are meant to be rivers and not lakes. We're meant to overflow to the outside. This is also so true of how churches are meant to be. Overflowing with life, vibrant, growing and fruitful. Not needy, inward-looking and sucking in energy like a black hole. Churches are on a mission to bless the world.

It reminds me of a passage in Luke's gospel, chapter 5 verses 1 to 11. Jesus is getting on with the work of preaching the gospel. Peter and friends have been fishing all night and have just dragged their nets in. They're tired and frustrated with nothing to show for all their effort. It also means no money and no food, so a few of these fruitless fishing trips can have big consequences. I'm sure they are in no mood for messing around. Even so Simon obeys the call of Jesus. Jesus doesn't call the crowds, He called the tired, busy fishermen. Doesn't Simon say yes to the call to catch people because he gets caught by Jesus? Leaving all their business, their lives, they followed Him. Peter, having met Jesus earlier with his brother, impetuously trusts Jesus was the promised Messiah. Leaving the world in faith, he steps forward and commits to Jesus. Letting go but gaining so much more. He began serving the Lord by standing in the water to hold the boat so He could speak.

From holding the boat to receiving an abundant haul of fish, to confession of his sinful heart before Jesus. Peter is face to face with the one who is overflowing, who fills all things.

> Jesus said to Simon, 'Do not be afraid; from now on you will be catching men.' And when they had brought their boats to land, they left everything and followed him (Luke 5: 10-11).

Peter does what the fish did, he responds to the voice of his creator. It's not, 'Jesus come and make my life a bit better', it's 'Jesus you are the Word of God'. And He tells them not to be afraid. They rightly fear Jesus, because of the realization of His immense love and fullness, His awesomeness. But He says, don't be afraid of me. Come and see what you will achieve, through my abundance and grace, when you follow me, I will use you to be fruitful through the gospel, cause life to flow through you. Make you a gatherer of the broken and downtrodden. Not through your efforts Peter, but through my abundance. Not because Peter is special, but because he obeyed and was humble. He responded to the call of the Lord.

So what did Peter and many of Jesus' followers do? Christian tradition tells us he gave his life for the gospel. He gave everything that he had for the kingdom without end, to a mission that is infinitely more fruitful. Instead of being successful in his business, he would be successful in the Church's business. When we say yes and follow Jesus, the possibilities are immense. Our lives become like a pleasant river flowing into this broken world. Where will God's mission take us? It is clear that we need to surrender and follow if we are to be fruitful and overflowing with life and blessing. It doesn't mean we all need to leave our homes and businesses to follow Jesus. For some it might, but, are we willing and ready to follow the Lord where He calls us? This is the overflowing life! Giving out to the needy and not hoarding.

Weight of Glory

> Do not take it, therefore, as an undoing, to lay up treasures in heaven, though you leave yourselves but little on earth. You lose no great advantage for heaven by becoming poor—in pursuing one's way, the lighter you travel, the better (Richard Baxter).[5]

Richard Baxter was the vicar of Kidderminster in England from 1647 to 1661. In his book *The Reformed Pastor*, he shares some practical and devotional advice to fellow ministers that I think is applicable to all Christians. He has some particular advice for church leaders though as setting the example to their congregations in how they live. He remarks what abundance of good ministers would do, if they would but live in contempt of the world, and its riches and glory. To expend all for the Lord's service, crucifying their own desires and greed, so they abound in cheerful generosity of love. It means whatever you

---

5   Richard Baxter, *The Reformed Pastor* (Edinburgh: Banner of Truth, 2001, 1862 Edition), p. 67.

have, you have for God. Baxter comments that this would unlock more hearts to the reception of the preaching and teaching of the pastor.

We Christians are not to invest in this life for ourselves, but sow intensely with every fibre into an eternal life with Christ we have already started living. The Bible says that we are to lay up treasures in heaven. The writer of the second letter to the church in Corinth, chapter 5, makes the comparison that our earthly home is like camping out in a tent. It's temporary living! No one would want to live constantly in a tent when you could have a house. Imagine living your life in a tent, you'd be groaning! Never going outside, when we look around all we see is the inside of this small tent. Our view is limited to the confines of the thin canvas. Living and storing up stuff in the tent isn't all that great when compared to God's amazing building prepared for us. We are to be living towards the future hope we have in Jesus, not living for today's temporary life in a tent.

Good works of charity are deposits for our future life with Christ in heaven. We don't get the benefit of them now, only the joyfulness of overflowing with all we have for God.

We don't work for our own salvation and resurrection, that's been given to us freely. Rewards are about our work for God, prepared by Him for us to do (Eph. 2:10), as empowered by the Spirit.[6] We do good works because of who we are in Christ and what we've already received, because of who God is. We make sacrifices for His sake. These good works of generosity are being registered by almighty God and follow us to heaven.

---

6   Randy Alcorn, *Heaven* (Wheaton, Illinois: Tyhdale House, 2004), p. 47.

Our reward for living faithfully will be an inheritance prepared by our Father in heaven. These are rewards from our good Father, like a parent rewarding a child for doing something for the first time.[7] As many parents would relate, God's rewards are helpful as a secondary motivation. We don't earn rewards; all such rewards are given entirely graciously by a loving Father who loves to give good gifts.

Future rewards help remind us that this world is temporary, it is pointless to try to grab onto things here and now. By not treasuring our wealth and property we can invest ourselves for God's kingdom. What we treasure is what we love. So to be cheerfully and profoundly generous means to focus on the important things here and now. We have the right perception of the thin canvas of life. This perspective will help us stand against Satan's snares. To quote Paul, 'For in this tent we groan, longing to put on our heavenly dwelling' (2 Cor. 5:2). We aren't to get too comfortable in the tent.

This life produces a weight of glory. After suffering comes glory, this is a pattern we see in the Bible.[8] God rewards His faithful workers with eternal treasure and authority rather than temporary rusting riches. The good news is that what is mortal shall be swallowed up by life. We're always looking to heaven. Whether you live in a palace or on the streets in a cardboard box, it's going to happen! One day there'll be no more mortality, and by the work of Jesus we shall enter eternity as royal heirs. We see and believe these things by faith

---

7   A.N.S. Lane, *Exploring Christian Doctrine* (London: SPCK, 2013), p. 220.

8   2 Corinthians 4:17.

and not by our eyes. Having received the down payment of the spirit now, we see a glimpse of Jesus now by the Spirit. Heaven is all about us gazing upon the face of Jesus, so we taste a little heaven now. When the tent, our earthly home, gets ripped apart, we know we have a building made by God in heaven full of promise, full of the glory of Jesus. Nothing can stop us getting to it if we are in Him. And, after the journey we can rest at last. Home.

If we cling onto our achievements and wealth like the rich young ruler in Mark 10, it shows that we are insecure and eventually we will inevitably lose the things we try to hold to. It will all fail and crumble. Doesn't all of human history teach us this truth? It's only by God's hands that we have anything to hold onto. If there's any security, safety, prosperity and satisfaction in this temporary life, it is only in and through the Lord Jesus.

You belong in Him, in heaven. Our dwelling has always been with the God who created us. You might start out working hard to succeed and generate wealth, success and security, but that's not where you're meant to stay dear friend. Those who are able to generate such wealth, must, in proportion to their talents, go beyond others. God has appointed a day, when He will judge the world in righteousness, by Jesus Christ. God the Father gives Him all the power and judgment to do this. Even Christians will need to give an account of their thoughts, words and deeds; and to receive according to what they have done in the body, whether good or evil.[9] Come Lord Jesus, come quickly.

---

9   Westminster Confession of Faith, 33, Of the Last Judgment.

4 Cheerful Givers Are Broken

Since all these things are thus to be dissolved, what sort of people ought you to be in lives of holiness and godliness? (2 Pet. 3:11)

From this glorious eternal vantage point, we view our lives on earth quite differently from the 'natural' short point of view. What sort of people are we to be? We don't often think it, but this temporary, tent-based life is a preparation for heaven. This is how the Bible frames it for us. We might not like this mindset, especially if we have a pretty cushy life now. It's easy to lose sight of the fact that we are pilgrims, passing through the toilsome wilderness to our promised land. Thankfully, this isn't our final destination. So then, does it matter how we behave in this life? Does the state of our hearts matter now, even though we are saved and going to heaven? Yes! We know from what the Bible teaches that our Creator cares deeply about our hearts in this life. Every moment of our lives matters, every moment matters forever. We may be saved and born again, but He wants us to grow and have pure hearts towards Him now and not just in heaven. Actually, the saved have already begun their new lives in Christ, for them eternity has already started and death is just a passing over. We are a people waiting for and hastening the coming of Jesus.

We live with heaven in view. With every moment mattering, we need to take care of our hearts, or they can be deceived. They can even be turned away from God, like King Solomon's, whose foreign wives enticed him away from following and loving the God of his father David. He should have listened to his own advice in Proverbs 4:23—'Keep your heart with all vigilance, for from it flow the springs of life'.

God is jealous for His glory and desires our whole heart be devoted to loving Him only. Only this gives joy and life. This is what we have been created for and this is the reality of the Trinity. He wants your heart, your love, desires and emotions, pointing to Him first and not split seven ways. Yet, when we do wander astray, He is the loving father running to welcome back the prodigal son. God's heart is full of love for Himself, passion for His glory and His name. But, He isn't an ego maniac and neither is He proud or demanding. It is simply the truth that He is altogether the loveliest and the most glorious person in existence. He just wants the very best for you, and that's who He is!

Hearts After God's Own Heart

In his book *Gentle and Lowly*, Dane Ortlund makes the point that Jesus' heart is gentle and lowly. He affirms that this is Christ's deepest heart for you. The Lord states it Himself in

Matthew 11. This also means that God's heart is gentle and lowly.[1] God's Son shows us what God's deepest heart is. He is accessible, and in all His shining glory it is easy to think of Jesus as associating with the very best, well educated, successful or famous. His overflowing life and love isn't just for some elite class, He is utterly approachable to us broken sinners. There's no one righteous anyway, only Him. He's gentle and lowly toward us because He loves us and wants us to share in His glory and life. We see it in how Jesus lives on earth, how He humbled Himself and turned none away. God's cheerful generosity is for everyone because He is gentle and lowly. He is a beautiful and winsome God, who welcomes sinners to come to Him and find rest.

> I have found in David the son of Jesse a man after my heart, who will do all my will (Acts 13:22).

As King David was a man after God's own heart, we too are to have this heart. Friends, this is more than cheerfully generous. When God's heart is gentle and lowly, it says more about Him than if He told us to be joyful and generous in heart. God doesn't need to be gentle or lowly does He? He's God. And yet He is. It is who He is, and it is what's bubbling up so readily. He is so affectionate to broken sinners. If this is God's heart, we too are to have this heart. We are to be accessible to those who perhaps we don't like to be around. Our generosity should also overflow from a gentle and lowly heart. There should not be any strings when we give.

---

1   Dane Ortlund, *Gentle and Lowly* (Wheaton, Illinois: Crossway, 2020), pp. 23, 26, 32.

We are not to lord it over people or manipulate others through giving. If we are gentle and lowly in heart like Jesus, then it needs to be reflected in the way we handle our money. We are to be accessible to the broken and lowly, open to help those who are in need and not shun them if at all possible. Quite often givers crave privacy and want to control who they are exposed to as givers. I get this motivation, I do, but if Jesus did this, half of His miracles wouldn't have happened. The lepers wouldn't have been healed nor would the blind and lame. They sought Him out and pleaded for mercy and forgiveness. He had compassion on them, wept for them. His great joy was to heal them and make them whole.

Our hearts direct and guide our actions. It's what defines who we are and what motivates us. What gives us the greatest joy? If our hearts are purely for God, like David, we'll love to do God's will. We'll have a godly posture that is humble and meek. If our life is in Christ then we must be meek and lowly like Jesus. This doesn't just happen overnight. We are transformed at conversion but we must also be shaped and reformed. It's a process! How we deal with money, decide how much to give, how and where to give, says something about the state of our hearts doesn't it?

What is the one thing that changes our hearts? It can only be the cross of Jesus. We see how He loves us, self-sacrificing, suffering, there on the cross. It captures our gaze and changes our hearts. Then we know deep down that Jesus really loves me. We know Jesus' heart is gentle and lowly because He loves even me. We come broken to the cross, sinners in need of saving. And, we need to keep coming back to the cross to be reminded we are not God's gifts. The truth is, we're broken failures and Christ loves us, as failures. When we see His great kindness we'll be moved as recipients of grace. Those of us who think of ourselves as donors, givers, philanthropists, shouldn't think of ourselves primarily as givers, we need to see ourselves as recipients of grace. That'll make us humble and gracious. It'll make us gentle and lowly, like Jesus. Our giving should be fuelled out of a response to His grace and His heart. Let's marvel at God's grace for a moment. God is so gracious with us isn't He? We see God's love in His graciousness to us. He treats us way better than we deserve. He is gracious and tender, slow to anger and kind. He gives grace and mercy beyond our dreams and hopes. No one can out-give God!

We give wrongly when we think it's out of our own power. That leads us down the wrong path completely. We think we're giving our money out of the goodness of our own hearts. No, we give of God's provision and as a recipient of His grace. This makes a profound difference to our hearts and motivations. It is the key to unlocking profoundly happy generosity in each of us.

What about receiving? I wonder how you respond to a generous gift? I often struggled with receiving gifts from others, not knowing how to deal with them and not really receiving them in my heart. In many ways it is harder to receive than to give. This sounds counter intuitive. I think as Christians it's especially true. When we give, we're in control. When we receive, we may fear strings being attached or a feeling of vulnerability. We might also feel a pressure to reciprocate. Godly receiving requires humility and grace. It goes back to the cross again, we are firstly recipients of grace. If you are a good receiver, you will be a rejoicing giver. Cheerful, humble and gracious.

Those who have suffered and been through difficult trials know the grace of God working in their lives. They personally know grace they have received, they have emotionally connected with, and experienced, the generosity of God in their time of need. These experiences make our faith more real and somehow enable us to better grasp what failures we are and how we need the Lord's grace and goodness. These precious times keep us near the cross. They remind us how dependent on Him we truly are! Without suffering, Christians can grow cold, proud, self-righteous and legalistic.

As a side note, this reminds me of the Apostle Paul's thorn in the flesh. God gave Paul a thorn in the flesh so he would not grow conceited. You might say, 'this is a strange gift to be given by a happy God overflowing with love.' It isn't strange if we see that God wants, and has plans for, our good. He wants to prosper us in His Son, for us to grow to become more like Him and not become comfortable in the world. He is preparing us for eternity in heaven and suffering is one of the ways through which God shapes us. Suffering, like having a metaphorical thorn in the flesh, is a kindness and generosity for our good. God will allow it and mean it for our good in His providence, to make us and shape us to become more like Jesus. Some of us are so gifted and reach such dizzying heights of success and acclaim, that we actually do need a thorn to prevent us growing prideful, puffed up and conceited. How many Christian leaders have fallen foul of pride and arrogance?

Money and power does often foster conceited and selfish hearts. I have seen leaders grow conceited with popularity and success—if only they'd have suffered a bit. The best leaders are those who have suffered. They are gentle and lowly. Suffering helps protect their hearts and avoid a prideful and painful fall.

So, is it wrong to want God's blessing and prosperity? To avoid suffering and pain?

The short account of Jabez found in 1 Chronicles is perhaps helpful to us as we think through prosperity.

> Jabez called upon the God of Israel, saying, 'Oh that you would bless me and enlarge my border, and that your hand might be with me, and that you would keep me from harm so that it might not bring me pain!' And God granted what he asked (1 Chron. 4:10).

Jabez was born in pain. That's what his name meant, his mother literally bore him in pain. We read that he was an honorable man and didn't want his name to be a bad omen for his life.

Jabez's prayer of faith shows us that a prayer for seeking prosperity, health and protection isn't wrong or a bad motive. It's a prayer of faith to the true God, he asks for God's blessing and that God's hand would be with him, that God would bless his efforts. God answered his heartfelt prayer. I'm not ashamed to say I've prayed this prayer in my life. Especially, when things haven't been going my way and I've felt abandoned and downtrodden. We cry out to the only one who can truly help us in our need. We know God is good and cheerfully generous, and He wants to bless us richly. Sadly, the prosperity movement is all about this, and see it as entitlement instead of a precious gift of God's grace.

All this is to say that cheerful givers are broken givers. They have been shaped by life's trials and suffering. But, they are not wallowing in self-pity or delighting in being miserable! Like the apostle Paul, they learn how to be brought low and how to abound, submitting to the providence of God for their lives. They are reminded by the cross that they are not God's gift, they are recipients of His grace. Their giving is a response to the grace of God and fuels their generosity all the more. They give because they have and are continually receiving of the kindness and goodness of God.

I just love the story of the poor widow's offering for the temple in Mark chapter 12. She was a broken giver. Jesus pointed her out to His followers as people came to give their offering to the temple treasury. Jesus valued her contribution more than the financially greater contributions of the wealthy, because she was a broken giver, sacrificially giving out of her poverty, not from the overflow of abundance. Christ knew that she had cheerfully put in all she had to live on, trusting in faith that the Lord would provide for her. Why does she do it?

No one would blame her for holding onto enough for food. She gives cheerfully from the overflowing love of God in her heart. Just like Jesus. Holding nothing back, because of love. The wealthy probably didn't even see her, but gentle and lowly Jesus sees her. We all need to be broken regardless of whether our status is abundance or poverty. This will allow us to give as recipients of God's grace and not think we are God's gift. This is important for us, for our delight in God and growth in Christ. It makes a profound difference to how we see 'our' money and belongings.

> Truly, I say to you, this poor widow has put in more than all those who are contributing to the offering box. For they all contributed out of their abundance, but she out of her poverty has put in everything she had, all she had to live on (Mark 12:43-44).

Two Broken Givers

Staying with the broken widow theme I want to pick out two broken women who were long-term patrons of extremely important ministries. One from the upper echelons of British society and one from the very bottom of the class ladder. Both broken, both totally committed to seeing the growth of the gospel. Being broken doesn't mean you have to be poor or have lived a life of hardship.

Lady Huntingdon was a prominent leader in the 18th-Century revival and a faithful patron of George Whitefield. Friend to John Wesley, she would correspond with him and Whitefield often. She certainly didn't hold to the same values as most in her class as part of England's nobility.[2] She didn't share the same pride or love of money, instead she felt grieved for the lost in her nation who had no thought of God. God had put this burden on her heart, the need in her land for the gospel. She was also a devoted wife and a mother, very happy in her marriage until Lord Huntingdon suddenly suffered a stroke and died leaving her with four children and a huge property portfolio at thirty-nine years of age. She suffered

2   J. Rinehart, p. 61.

much with two more sons dying of smallpox, but it proved to be a pivotal point in her life. The countess had come to realize that she was nothing, in spite of her status and money. She had come to a place of brokenness; Jesus Christ had become all.[3]

This new condition allowed greater freedom to follow the Lord as a recipient of grace. She visited Wales and joined a preaching tour with the evangelist Howell Harris. She had experienced the fire of revival there as the Spirit convicted people of their need of a Savior. Her only aim now was for Christ to be preached all over the world. Lady Huntingdon reached out to Whitefield to propose a partnership. She realized she had received status and position in the aristocracy, now she wanted to use that totally for God's purpose. She held preaching meetings at her home for royalty, politicians and the upper class. Lady Huntingdon endorsed Whitefield, thus greatly helping to further his cause and open more doors for revival across the nation. She devoted her entire fortune to the work of the gospel, building 116 church buildings throughout England's cities to supply the demand for places for worship. She also built a seminary in Wales in Howell Harris' hometown to help train more pastors and provided generous scholarships for their upkeep.[4]

There is something truly beautiful here for us to pause and ponder. There are many such stories of generous philanthropists actively partnering with pastors and church leaders in movements of God through the ages. I suspect though, not

---

3   Ibid, p. 66-67.
4   Ibid, p. 85.

as many as might be. Here we see a potent and powerful partnership of reformation and revival. Perhaps you are a Lady Huntingdon reading this chapter, dream with me if you will about what God might achieve through you in this age. I often hear the term 'kingdom return'. Oh, that the Lord would achieve something without measure of return through you as a patron of a Whitefield! I challenge you, to seek out a George Whitefield and work together, get involved and become invested. Don't just join some boards of successful ministries and give when they implore you. Help finance them and help them achieve what it is the Lord is calling them to do for His glory. If God is in it, why do we see ministries and churches struggling for funds when He has provided adequately for His work?

I believe this was the Lady's mindset and drive. This is how seriously she took her role in the mission. She was given the influence, connections, education and financial means by the Lord to supercharge Whitefield's ministry and the Methodist movement. Both Britain and America were transformed and hugely impacted with the gospel because of this partnership in a time of spiritual wilderness. I challenge you reading this: if God has given you the means and influence, seek out your George Whitefield and commit everything to that calling! If you hoard and find security in your treasure, that's where your small heart will be. It will be an obstacle to your spiritual growth and a misuse of the Lord's provision.

I grew up in a little village in the Neath valley in Wales. My earliest memories are of packed Sunday services in the little Clyne Free Mission that was established as a mission to miners. The chapel was a corrugated steel and wood construction that was built by Glyn Vivian of the Vivian family from Swansea. Along with my home church, he established missions in Swansea, Japan and around the world, recruiting pastors and financing the work. The Vivian family were copper magnates in Swansea. The chapel in my village burned brightly for the gospel when other churches had closed. I remember hearing the voices of the miners singing revival hymns and hearing first-hand experience of the 1904 revival. Lord, may those days return to the valleys of Wales! Where are the next Glyn Vivians of today?

If you are reading this and you're thinking that you aren't a wealthy Huntingdon or a Vivian, I want to take you back to George Müller's poor needlewoman—a hard-working lady who was invested in Müller's ministry from the beginning. Her gifts were as costly as Lady Huntingdon's, in spite of the vast difference in amounts. Remember this poor needlewoman initially brought a one hundred pound gift from an inheritance, a great deal of money at the time. As Müller checked her motives, her reply convinced him fully, 'The Lord Jesus has given his last drop of blood for me, and should I not give him this hundred pounds?' These supporters are wonderful encouragements and means of grace to ministries. The hundred pounds was seed funding for the beginning of the orphan work. Müller had partnership with the lady throughout his ministry. She was all in. She didn't have a public profile, in fact only less than half a dozen people knew of her faithful patronage. She gave food, clothing and money to the poor. Gifts contributed were so above her means that her resources were quickly depleted.[5]

---

5   A.T. Pierson, *George Müller of Bristol*, pp. 326-327.

Our natural instinct would be to try to talk her out of bringing gifts that she could not afford, as was Müller's. Once he could see her act of love of Jesus, giving out of the grace she had received how could he deny her cheerful generosity? She gave humbly and secretly, pouring everything she could give to support the ministry, trusting in the providence of God to provide and keep her. And, you know what? God did. After her money was gone and she could no longer work to support herself God wonderfully provided for her, so she was never left to want. She asked for no help from people, only making her appeal to the Lord. He more than provided and comforted her even in great suffering, she was filled with praises for Him.

This is the kind of radical generosity that sows transformation that changes the world. Such is the impact of this kind of partnership that we know the names and the stories centuries later. The legacy of faith-driven vision, joyful sacrifice and gospel patronage makes far reaching impact. William Tyndale and Humphrey Monmouth, John Newton and John Thornton, and more recently another wealthy widow, Mr.s. Dora Hillman and R.C. Sproul.

The motivation of these givers wasn't to influence or play God, neither was it so they'd have a lasting legacy for decades. No, they give out of the grace they have received, driven by love for Christ and treasuring what lay ahead in eternity, the love of Christ compelling them to be cheerfully generous with the reassurance that they can give all away in the knowledge of the providence of God for their good.

5 Playing God

> Have this mind among yourselves, which is yours in Christ Jesus, who, though he was in the form of God, did not count equality with God a thing to be grasped, but emptied himself, by taking the form of a servant, being born in the likeness of men. And being found in human form, he humbled himself by becoming obedient to the point of death, even death on a cross (Phil. 2:5-8).

For a moment, think of someone like a Kim Jong Un, the leader of North Korea. He presents himself to his people as a living god. I think he personifies what some people think God is like. A tyrannical, self-centered, dictator. A deified mob boss ruling the population through fear. Completely self-absorbed, unloving and insecure. It's not actually a big stretch to think a character like Kim could run a country. It can happen even in our time, if we understand the wickedness the human heart is capable of. Enabled to be like Kim, we might end up just like him if we had absolute power and control of a country. This is in the spirit of anti-Christ.

Though not dictators, we do like to act or think that we are our own little gods: gods of our own lives with absolute sovereignty over ourselves. Well, here's a newsflash, Jesus is God. Not in the sense of Kim Jong Un, but being very God Himself. When He came among mankind, He didn't present Himself like Kim. He wasn't born in a grand palace. He chose to be born in a cattle stable in the feeding trough, in a backwater town. Having the power of God at His fingertips and everything at His command, yet didn't use it for Himself, He didn't hold onto it for His own enjoyment.

At the time appointed, He humbled Himself, embracing the shame of the cross. This is what the exercise of true power looks like. Jesus' attitude of equality with God was to serve others, even painfully to death. This is the supreme demonstration of who God is and His attitude to power and wealth. God is overflowing and giving out of Himself, not hoarding and storing up. Not simply giving from His abundance, but sacrificially giving His all, out of love.

In his letter to the Philippian church, Paul is saying that we are to have the same attitude as Jesus towards power, wealth and status. Power isn't given to us in order to get more, but to serve and give away to others. Jesus emptied Himself and took the form of a servant. For example, you're not given financial power to get more wealth for yourself and your family. This is quite often the trap we fall into. If we do use this God-given power to get more for ourselves, to hoard it all up, then it is an abuse of the power and resources that God has given us. It can become a snare to us. Everything we are and have been given, all our time, energy and talents are given by God to glorify

Him. To bless others—not for us to use to make ourselves more powerful, wealthy or comfortable. It is meant for His glory not our glorification. Unfortunately, not everyone got the memo.

Jonathan Edwards, a pastor during the 18th Century's Great Awakening in America said, 'True faith mostly depends on having the emotions of God, loving the things He loves.'[1] God does not take comfort and joy in worldly things. Perhaps at times our suffering is severe but we are still called to sacrificially give of ourselves. How can we do this? Edwards would say we can only do it because our spiritual joy is greater than our suffering and hardship, this joy from Christ supports and enables us to suffer and give cheerfully.[2] Joy that is unspeakable and full of glory.

We naturally don't have big hearts overflowing with love and generosity. This is why the global 1% controls 45% of the world's wealth (according to Oxfam's 2019 report). I'm not arguing for a socialist worldview here! One where wealth is taken away from you and distributed to others. No, far from it, that isn't generosity. The call of this book is the life of discipleship, of following Christ. It is one of giving of self to others. The Bible takes it further, it says that this is life! The overflow of love to others. To be like our servant king. To avoid living like Him as His disciples is futile and self-destructive. Sinful!

---

1   Jonathan Edwards, *Religious Affections*, p. 22 (modern rendering).

2   Ibid, p. 21.

I realize that this won't apply to everyone, but there's another pitfall you could fall into. If you have been given the ability to give generously, you could play God in your giving. You don't use wealth to hoard up for yourself but instead you trade it for influence and power over others. Wealthy givers lacking the great commission compass can also negatively impact churches and ministries in a particular country or across a whole region by choosing what they give to and what they don't give to. Trust fund managers can play politics, preferring to fund specific ministries over others for alternative motives, to align with success or favoritism. This is also playing god with the Lord's money, and they'll have to give account for how they have stewarded what God has entrusted to them. Friends, if you think you're the fount of all giving, you are playing God. In contrast, if you know in your heart that you're a redeemed failure, you know you've been shown such generosity then you'll be like God, not playing Him to others—truly cheerful and open-handed in your generosity. Joy will come through giving because it is gracious giving not a transaction for power, politics or influence. We are recipients of such grace, we give out of what we have received from God.

I put it to you that giving a few resources from the overflow of our abundance is a litmus test of our Christianity and faith. It shows that you don't get the gospel. Are you giving some stuff you can spare or are you giving yourself? By giving yourself, it doesn't mean giving up being a CEO or owner of a family business. You don't need to stop what you're doing and go join a missionary agency. What it means is that you are not being a business owner for yourself, but for the Lord. It means giving all your gifts to Him, giving everything to Him. This will change the way you do business and how you treat your employees. Jesus gives Himself away. This is the life Jesus calls us to, as we join Him on the Calvary way. He might call some of us to give all of ourselves away, even our very lives. But don't worry about losing comfort and security, Jesus has prepared a place for you, a place that is more secure and eternally lasting.

In the 16th century, William Tyndale's friend and patron, Humphrey Monmouth, ended up imprisoned in the Tower of London because he partnered with Tyndale in his English Bible translation. This work was central to seeding the English Reformation. The risks were high and both men went into the project counting the cost. I visited the Tower of London this year with my family and remember seeing where Walter Raleigh was held. I remember seeing the Traitor's Gate where the convicted were taken into the heavily fortified fortress. It was a place out of which those convicted didn't often walk. Conditions in the Tower were extremely harsh for prisoners. After a year, Monmouth walked out of the Tower but soon heard of Tyndale's execution in Belgium.[3] They were all in for the Reformation. They gave everything for the cause of the gospel and reaped an eternal reward in Christ.

When Giving Is in My Interest

Historical figures are great examples for helping us think about generosity and stewardship, because we have lost our way in the modern age. We have been influenced by our culture and

---

3   J. Rinehart, pp. 48-51.

postmodern independent thought and consumerism. The results are clear to see in that the way we deal with our money and generosity is an afterthought. As a ministry leader and one that engages regularly with raising ministry support, I know how the American people are renowned for their amazing generosity. I've experienced first-hand the great hospitality and generosity while visiting friends.

If you have been fundraising in the U.S. you'd know Year-End giving is a particular flurry of fundraising activity because it is the end of the U.S. Tax year. Many people are thinking and praying about where to give their tax efficient donations. However, I want to put it to my American friends that giving to support ministry merely for tax deduction reasons and perhaps out of duty, isn't really generosity. U.S. Taxes are set up to stimulate ungenerous giving as a function of a household or business tax deduction. Don't get me wrong, its fantastic for the charity sector. Here's an interesting statistic: charitable giving by individuals in America fell 1.1% to $292 billion in 2018, according to Giving USA. The decline in giving by individuals came after a new tax law, which took effect in 2018, reduced the tax incentives for giving for many households.[4] The amount given to charity by Americans was directly affected by a change in the law reducing the incentives to give to charity. So, giving went down, showing that many were only giving in order to gain a tax deduction. Having said that, I do know many Americans who are incredibly and

---

4   https://www.cnbc.com/2019/06/18/charitable-giving-dropped-last-year-in-the- wake-of-the-new-tax-law.html

cheerfully generous. They give in spite of the tax incentives, to the point of profound generosity.

In America, this is just what people do because there are such incentives. It's in the culture, and it is remarkable that it is. But, when Christians are doing the same thing in the same way and not giving of themselves, giving for tax efficiency to Christian ministry, it isn't counter-cultural or loving, though I'm sure it's of big impact for those recipient churches and ministries. You might also be playing God when you divide up your tax-deductible donations, giving from your excess. You might sit down at the end of the year and think, now where shall I put my money? Who is deserving of the stuff I have to give away? See, you're not giving of yourself because your heart's not changed. Your decision is based on a financial equation not a heart's joyful outpouring. Dear friend, there is so much more you can gain. I'm sure everyone else from other countries can draw parallels with your context.

Christian, be profoundly generous. Whatever your status and affluence, class or family and tax system. You won't be robbing yourself of happiness, you'll be robbing yourself of being joyless. Why imprison yourself in reluctance? Why settle for safety, security or comfort? Be cheerful! You won't find joy in your wealth, cars and houses. It's never too late to change our hearts, Christ delights in showing us mercy. Let's come to Him like blind Bartimaeus and not like the rich young ruler.

> And Jesus, looking at him, loved him, and said to him, 'You lack one thing: go, sell all that you have and give to the poor, and you will have treasure in heaven; and come, follow me.'

> Disheartened by the saying, he went away sorrowful, for he had great possessions (Mark 10:21-22).

No, let's not go away from the Lord disheartened because we have great possessions, status and influence. He would never turn us away. Instead, we jump up from our comfort and security and fly to Christ for mercy. Like the poor blind beggar, Bartimaeus:

> But he cried out all the more, 'Son of David, have mercy on me!' And Jesus stopped and said, 'Call him.' And they called the blind man, saying to him, 'Take heart. Get up; he is calling you.' And throwing off his cloak, he sprang up and came to Jesus (Mark 10:48-50).

Jesus invites the rich young man to follow Him, but he decides he can't and goes away sad. Christ didn't ask the beggar to follow Him, but he does so even though he had received his sight. To follow Christ on the way means emptying ourselves and taking the form of a servant. The trappings of success tempt us to not need Christ, we fill ourselves and make others serve us. We provide for ourselves and do not look to God for provision. This robs us of joy because it robs us of Christ. We can find genuine pleasure in Christlike generosity. But this can't be unless our hearts are changed. Jesus invites you to follow Him, what will your reaction be?

Don't play God, give all to God.

Humble Generosity

> Beware of practising your righteousness before other people in order to be seen by them, for then you will have no reward

from your Father who is in heaven. Thus, when you give to the needy, sound no trumpet before you, as the hypocrites do in the synagogues and in the streets, that they may be praised by others. Truly, I say to you, they have received their reward. But when you give to the needy, do not let your left hand know what your right hand is doing, so that your giving may be in secret. And your Father who sees in secret will reward you (Matt. 6:1-6).

Jesus teaches His disciples how they are to give to the poor and needy in the Sermon on the Mount. Money is one of the subjects Jesus teaches on most. Jesus teaches that in God's eyes, giving to help the poor and needy is an act of righteousness. Christians are meant to do acts of righteousness, motivated by love as unto Christ. These are precious acts of kindness to be done humbly and not for us to be seen to receive praise from people like the Pharisees. Jesus taught His followers how to live as citizens of the kingdom of heaven. Life in a present and future reality. He spoke about how to deal with anger, lust, divorce, prayer, money... and giving. Giving generously is an act of cheerful overflowing love that is also an act of righteousness. The problem is we want others to see our righteousness, to see how 'good we are'.

Hypocrites love to put on a good show to make people think they are so good and generous. They're having their reward for their righteousness now. For them, righteous deeds like giving to the poor and needy are all an act. It's purely a transaction. Present glory and status in return for money and good works. Jesus calls them whitewashed tombs. Sparkly and flashy on the outside, rotten and corrupt on the inside. Jesus is calling out attention-seeking givers as hypocrites. They give in order to be seen by others. This is their motivation to give, and their immediate reward. It isn't a cheerful generosity, but a sad self-glorifying attempt to make one's heart cheerful. To be one's own god. Desiring to be adored and loved, seeking joy from others instead of from God, the source of joy.

But is it wrong to speak about your own giving? The only time I think it is right is when the motive is to encourage cheerful generosity in others and not show off your own righteousness. This should be encouraged because we simply don't talk about money or generosity at all these days. We can be humbly generous and also challenge others to join us, for their joy and practice of righteousness. It is good to share about your giving in the right way and with the right motive, and also to model what humble generosity looks like. The practice of righteousness is a regular discipline and should be done without fanfare. We who are in Jesus are to give with quiet humility. Not drawing attention to the act, but to actively avoid receiving praise back. We are to give as if we're not even aware of what we're doing or seeing the weight of our action, knowing our audience is our 'Father who sees in secret' and He will reward us.

How can cheerfulness be secret? It sounds counter-intuitive. Our giving doesn't need to be shouty or showy to be cheerful, because our cheerfulness comes from the deep well of living water we have within from God. We can't buy lasting cheerfulness through giving to the needy like the Pharisees. They give to hear the praise of others, rather than God. They go after the favor of men by their giving but also by their ostentatious prayers. Giving is like prayer, when done in secret, it is done for God. God is near to us in our affections; therefore we can pray and give quietly and secretly and know God's approval in it. We pray to our Father in secret, that our Father who is in secret, may hear us. We give in secret, that our Father who is in secret, may reward us in secret.[5]

If being prayer-less is a barrier to cheerful generosity, so too is greed. Greed is a major blockage to generosity. Greed is taking in, generosity is giving out. Many of us probably aren't aware of it until we come face to face with the monster. Greed is so destructive, changing people and eroding integrity and character. It is the polar opposite to contentment and cheerful generosity and makes us discontented and as miserable as sin.

Greed means always prioritizing one's own comfort and good over and above everyone else. Unchecked, it is an unquenchable thirst for money or stuff to have gratification, status and joy. Greed never wants to give away, it is a relentless hoarder, ever building bigger storehouses.

Greed stems from the unbridled love of wealth and is the fruit of the fear of losing security and comfort. A greedy heart is not a content heart, always wanting more and never contented. Drunk on the love of money.

> Keep your life free from the love of money, and be content with what you have, for he has said 'I will never leave you or forsake you' (Heb. 13:5).

---

5   John Calvin, *Institute of the Christian Religion*, (1536 edition, Translated by Ford Lewis Battles, London: Collins Liturgical Publications, Revised Edition 1986), p. 74.

The Lord is our helper and provider. Do we believe it? Do we really trust the Lord's good provision, or do we trust ourselves? If we trust Him for the salvation of our eternal soul, why look to ourselves for our life on earth? The Lord has provided for us in salvation through the giving of His own blood. He will continue to provide for us through this life so we ought not to fear and prioritize security but choose to be profoundly generous. Choose to be happy and contented completely in the Lord Jesus. Self-denial is critical in the life of a Christian, we need to oppose our vanity not encourage it. Pick up our cross and follow Jesus.

In his book on contentment, Jeremiah Burroughs offers us a great description of contentment:

> Christian contentment is that sweet, inward, quiet, gracious frame of spirit, which freely submits to and delights in God's wise and fatherly disposal in every condition.[6]

He goes on to say how contentment is a work of the Holy Spirit in our hearts, sweetening our inner life. Greed comes from our sin and desire; contentment is from God. It means not only not helping ourselves, but also forbearing from discontentment and murmuring against God and others. Do you find yourself doing this under your breath? Putting on a Christian mask, but inwardly roaring with grumblings and discontentment. Are you giving yourself a pass because it's not harming anyone? But it is harming your heart. Contentment is the inward submission of the heart. Are we able to join with

---

6   Jeremiah Burroughs, *The Rare Jewel of Christian Contentment* (1651 Edition, Edinburgh: Banner of Truth, 1964), p. 19.

King David in Psalm 62:1, by saying, 'For God alone my soul waits in silence'? In his formative years, David knew what it meant to wait on and for God. He wouldn't make a move without knowing the Lord was with Him.

Being wealthy and prosperous is a great burden which can rob you of contentment and bring you harm. Who'd think that being wealthy was a burden?! Few ask the question, 'Can I bear this great burden and duty?' If you find yourself coming into a great deal of money, and don't plan on how you are going to steward this resource, then you are in for a great deal of trouble. You need to have a strong spirit to bear the weight of wealth. If someone's drive is to become rich, this can bring much sorrow. The heart likes to dwell on the many outward delights, but does not consider the deep sorrows which will pierce the heart[7] (1 Tim. 6: 10). I'm sure that you have looked on the prosperity of someone and thought, 'I wish I was that guy'. If we only knew the troubles that he was dealing with in his family, his possessions and business dealings, we'd see quite a different perspective. Being prosperous also brings a great deal of danger. People who are set on a pedestal are in more danger than others are. A prosperous person attracts danger like honey attracts bees. People with money attract unwanted attention from those who want it, from the Devil and temptation. The dangers that prosperous men face are more than others in a more humble position. A great many more temptations.

---

7   Ibid, pp. 103-109.

A Christian Duty

Being wealthy means you have a duty to God. This can be an unforeseen burden. Having the means to help the poor means that you have a Christian duty to God, not to perform grudgingly, but a duty to be enjoyed. God commands His people to be freely generous to the poor in Deuteronomy chapter 15. It is a constant requirement because we will always have the poor with us. Those who have been blessed with much, might seem to be in a pretty cushy situation, but often don't consider the duty they have to God. To whom much has been given, from him much will be required (Luke 12:48). You might crave status, the house, the Bentley and swimming pool? But can you bear the duty expected? At the last day, we all must give an account to God for what we have done on earth. We are all stewards aren't we? Jeremiah Burroughs says, 'Those who are in a high and prosperous condition have annexed to it the burden of trouble, of danger, of duty, and of account.'

I'm not trying to convince you to give away all of your earthly possessions because that will make you happy. But the Lord does want us to be content in Him. Christians should be content because God has blessed us in Christ with every spiritual blessing in the heavenly places. Not, in the earthly treasure houses. We won't necessarily see tangible blessings on earth, but we will most assuredly see tangible blessings in heaven as a present reality. Those blessings are completely full up. Every possible spiritual blessing can only be found by us being 'in' Christ. What is our response to this?

Let men give as liberally as they may, you can always proclaim the value of their gift: you can cast it up, and reckon its worth; but God's gift is unspeakable, unreckonable. You cannot fully estimate the value of what God gives. The gospel is a gospel of giving and forgiving. We may sum it up in those two words; and hence, when the true spirit of it works upon the Christian, he forgives freely, and he also gives freely. The large heart of God breeds large hearts in men, and they who live upon his bounty are led by his Spirit to imitate that bounty, according to their power (Charles Haddon Spurgeon).[8]

How do we thank God for His unspeakable gift? Thank Him by doing something to prove your thankfulness. We can excuse ourselves of this by waiting for the ideal situation, something that ticks our giving priorities boxes. What does it say about our gratitude that we give God the thanks and glory with words but fail to show it with kindness? We have large hearts to love Christ and to love Christ's poor people. It's a good place to start and should be an easy place to start. We put our money where our mouth is. If we get into good disciplines early, as we receive the Lord's most valuable gift, then we will continue to respond practically to testify of our salvation.

---

8   C. H. Spurgeon, Sermon, 27th July, 1890, 'Praise for the Gift of Gifts'.

6 Conclusion

Blessed be the God and Father of our Lord Jesus Christ, who has blessed us in Christ with every spiritual blessing in the heavenly places (Eph. 1:3).

Our theology drives and informs our generosity. If our view of God is cold, fearful and limiting, then that's what our generosity will be like! If our view of God is as the Father who chose us before the world, who pours His love and mercy through His Son to us, then we too will overflow. The love of the Father isn't changeable or clenched, it is like the care of a mother hen to her young chicks who take shelter under her wings. This then is the question I want to put to you: to whom does God want to overflow through you?

God proves the gospel in us through good works like serving others, giving money and sacrificing to help others. This is what validates what we are preaching with our mouths. Every day God is breathing through us. This packs more of a punch than merely good works alone. These love works are driven by the gospel and the love of God. We don't need to make ourselves do this grudgingly, it is the natural overflow of our life in Christ as He gave of Himself to us. The world will want the Church to divorce the gospel from good works. 'Do good works, just don't preach that stuff anywhere'. We start becoming ashamed of the good news. Friends, it is impossible to separate the gospel from good works without changing the very essence of the good stuff you want to be doing. For Christians, we do good things like financially supporting our local church ministry because we are in Christ and we believe and love the gospel.

Let's get practical. What makes me want to give money sacrificially to my local church or ministry? Giving your own hard-earned money sacrificially is putting your money where your mouth is. Proving the gospel. So, what about tithing? Tithing is a tenth part of something like your income. As far as I'm concerned, it is the minimal amount we should be generously giving. Biblically, there's nothing to say it is no longer relevant. It is a helpful guide, but we should be exceeding this amount like the people of Israel in the Old Testament. As believers we are no longer under the Mosaic covenant, because Christ reformed the covenant to give us a better one. I would say that we are not required to tithe like the Jews, but we are required to give more generously than the law would have us. At the same time, we're not going to be cursed or judged for not tithing.

The good works or fruit are important, the overflowing of generosity, the charity, but why? The Bible tells us in James that faith without works is a dead faith. A living faith in Jesus is an overflowing faith, it is dynamic and living, and it has an active product now. As Spurgeon said, 'The large heart of God breeds large hearts in people'. We are blessed in Christ with every spiritual blessing, what a bounty! We want to imitate this overflow of blessings to others as we are able. We're all convinced we need to give, but let's do some self-reflection and look inside our hearts.

Happy vs Hesitant Giving

I found Mark Dillon's book helpful to place different types of givers in four profiles.[1] Mark's book is written primarily for people raising money for ministries. He makes the point that not all givers are the same and there are at least four kinds of givers. I would agree with his analysis, and I have adapted his profiles and changed them slightly for the purposes of this book. This generosity spectrum is relevant to all Christians not just fundraisers, I include it for self-reflection. Christians should aim to move from the reluctant to the cheerful, if you're not there already. The differences in the generosity spectrum have nothing to do with how much people are able to give away.

THE RELUCTANT GIVER

- There's no theology or model for generous giving
- 'It's my money, my business'
- Irritated to be asked to give
- Doesn't want to engage with the needy directly

---

1   R.M. Dillon, *Giving & Getting in the Kingdom: A Field Guide* (Chicago: Moody Publishers, 2012), pp. 45-49.

- Frequently finds fault and finds reasons not to give

Mark makes the point that this category of giver represents as much as a third of a church congregation or of the supporters of a Christian organization.[2] There can be many environmental or behavioral reasons why someone might be in this category and doesn't move on. It's where we all start—the entry level of giving. I would argue that the overwhelming reason why someone is a reluctant giver is because they have no theology of generosity. Sadly, they don't really know how generous God is to them and why.

THE GIVER WHO PLAYS GOD

- Gives only what they can spare
- Gives simply for tax reasons
- Tends to tip God
- 'How much of my money should I give to God?'
- Usually needs to be persuaded to give

This giver has a small view of God because they have a big view of themselves. They think they're the fount of all giving and it shows. They don't have a big heart for Christ's needy people. They don't know in their heart that they're a redeemed failure and have been shown such generosity. The result is clenched, closed-handed generosity.

THE THOUGHTFUL GIVER

- Aware of God's call on their life
- 'How much of God's money shall I give?'

---

2   Ibid, p. 49.

- Usually needs to be asked
- Experiences satisfaction in the act of giving
- Thinks that giving is a 'good thing to do'

This giver can experience the joy of giving but perhaps doesn't know why. It can perhaps be transactional instead of being a transformative motive. They know God's call on their life but stick to a measured amount connected with their income. It rarely involves hardship and leaving themselves short because of sacrificial giving.

THE REJOICING GIVER

- Profoundly aware of God's call on their life and possessions
- 'How much of God's money should I keep?'
- Experiences great joy in giving
- Seldom need to be asked
- They feel that if they aren't obedient in giving then they're not following Christ.

Here is a Christian after God's own heart. Who can't help but overflow with rejoicing generosity? When we think about philanthropy, what do we think? That it's a word only for rich people who have the means? Philanthropy is defined as the love of mankind. It is said that Christian philanthropy enables us to love God through loving mankind. I think this is fundamentally backwards thinking. If we flip that statement to, Christian philanthropy is our love of God enabling us to love mankind, then this better theology helps fuel our generosity aright. It will help us become rejoicing givers.

Where would you put yourself on the generosity spectrum? I pray that you are challenged at this point to review your giving and your own heart. Can you put your hand on your heart and say I am a rejoicing giver? The Bible encourages us to seek growth in maturity to godliness, it calls it 'growing up in Christ'. Ensuring we are growing does mean we need to somehow measure our growth in Christ. I remember my father measuring my height as a boy by drawing a pencil line on a door frame. He would repeat this every month, and, sure enough, I could see my own physical growth after a few months. I put it to you that generosity is a similar spiritual measurement that we can observe in ourselves. Generosity is the pencil line on God the Father's door frame, by it, we see the fruit of the Spirit. By it, we see if we live and walk by the Spirit. We and others see the visible evidence that we belong to Christ, that we have received the Father's gift only by grace, only through faith in Jesus.

Why should we change? Most people like feeling safe and comfortable. We can fear change, can't we? Change feels risky and we shy away from risk. It's easy to seek comfort and security in money and stuff. You might think, 'I have my salvation, I've got my ticket to heaven and I can settle back, seek safety and enjoy the ride'. But do you fear God? Does He factor in your decisions? The truth is we should fear God instead of people and circumstances. If we love God as God, our love is a fearful love because He is God. We tremble at His compassion and magnificence. This unpopular truth is a cure for worldliness, the Bible says that the fear of the Lord is the beginning of wisdom and knowledge. That's a good reason to change. The fear of the Lord helps us overcome our fear of risk.

In Michael Reeves' book *Rejoice and Tremble*,[3] he makes the point that as we rejoice and tremble at who God is, it gives us the wisdom and strength we need to live. We shouldn't fear or be in dread. Let God be your fear rather than fearing loss of security, comfort or money. Then you'll live freely in Christ.

> For God gave us a spirit not of fear but of power, love and self-control (2 Tim. 1:7).

In this text, fear can be better translated as timidity, or perhaps cowardice, or weakness and shame. Our God does not want us to live like this. To be safe and comfortable in our wealth and property makes us fearful of losing them. We can't operate in the gifts God has given us or the power of His Spirit if we are bound by this fear. The gifts and resources are there in full, don't choose cowardice and security over being all in for Christ. Fear handicaps us, it isn't a gift from God. He's given us the resources to do the exact opposite.

Fuelling Gospel Work

What can be achieved when cheerful generosity is coupled with a fearless vision for God's kingdom? John Pugh was a railway worker who became a minister in South Wales, UK, in the late 1800s. He was a man greatly used by God among others to see a great revival in Wales and he founded the 'Forward Movement' (a missions movement). This was a church

---

3   Michael Reeves, *Rejoice and Tremble* (Wheaton, Illinois: Crossway, 2021).

movement to reach English-speaking people in South Wales, lots of newcomers having arrived from England and Ireland to work in the mines and factories. The Movement began amidst the harsh reality of social deprivation in a borrowed tent on some waste ground. In fifteen years it had built forty-eight church buildings seating 43,080 people, 10,763 children in the Sunday Schools and had thirty evangelists serving South Wales.[4]

As the Lord raised up Huntingdon for Whitefield, he raised up John Cory and David Davies for John Pugh and the Forward Movement. Davies and Cory were two entrepreneurs responsible for the industrialization of South East Wales. They built Barry Docks as an alternative to the expensive and congested Cardiff docks in order to export coal from their coal mines in the South Wales Valleys, even transporting the coal to the docks by their own Taff Vale railway. The village of Barry grew from fewer than a hundred people to a seaport of over 30,000. By 1913 the docks were the greatest coal exporter in the world! As you would expect, these developments brought enormous social changes and needs for the growing population. Both Davies and Cory passionately supported Pugh's vision of reaching anglicized families of the men who worked for them in the docks and down the coal mines.[5] These captains of industry cared deeply for the souls of their workers and were ready to give generously.

---

4   G. Fielder, *Grace, Grit and Gumption*, p. 13.

5   Ibid, p. 11.

This is a story that hits close to home for me, as I'm from the valleys where the coalfields were. I know many of the Forward Movement churches and grew up hearing the names John Pugh, Frank and Seth Joshua who led it, and heard about their exploits. As I look back I can see how churches in South Wales have been shaped by these characters. Both my grandfathers were coal miners and probably worked in the very mines owned by Cory. I've spent many hours at Dyffryn House with my family, where John Cory lived. That's where Pugh had his first meeting with John and Richard Cory:

> John Cory invited us to spend the last evening of 1891 in his beautiful home. He invited us to place our scheme to evangelize the masses before him. Our simple but practical scheme so commended itself to his clear head and warm heart, that he there and then promised us his generous support.

In his book, *Grace, Grit and Gumption*, Geraint Fielder comments how with modern government having to look to private sector funding for many amenities, we remember these Victorian masters of industry who funded such great philanthropic work caring for the spiritual and physical needs of the people. It is a striking testimony to us today of great gospel partnership, integrity, evangelical faith and profound generosity. It is recorded that John Cory was regularly giving £50,000 per year to churches and evangelical movements. In today's money that is nearly £6,000,000! We are all called to give generously and cheerfully to the Lord's work—rich and poor, working class or nobility—as the Lord has enabled us to give, to resource gospel work to build God's kingdom.

Esteeming the Church

So, perhaps we have the motive and conviction to change. Now, where do we focus our generosity? There's no doubt that as Christians, we should be giving to our local church. It is just a given if you know what the Bible says about the local church. It is the assembly of believers with whom we meet to worship, pray and hear the Word of God preached.

Ministries are also worthy recipients as the Spirit moves your heart to a particular cause. However, let's remember that the Church is the only organization on earth that God has said He will bless. In Matt 16:18, Jesus says He will build His Church, continuing the pattern established by God in the Old Testament. Calling people to Himself to be a worshiping assembly.

There are those who say that ministries and Christian organizations are all together part of the Church. That is true in the sense that all Christians everywhere, in secular work, charities and churches are all part of the universal body of Christ. But the Bible is clear about what Church is and what Church isn't. Functionally, 'Para-church' or servant ministries aren't the local church, they're organizations created by founders to carry out a particular mission. The Church has been gathered and organized by God to carry out the great commission.

Gathered to worship and make more worshipers. Ministries are under the Church and are there to serve the

Church, that she be fit for Christ. They provide resources to help the Church in fulfilling the Great Commission of Jesus. This is an important point and should be reflected in our giving priorities and will help guard against playing God with giving. When servant ministries try to do the work of the local church and even work around the local church it is dysfunctional and no good will come of it. I am often struck by how servant ministries that are authentically committed to the flourishing of the Church tend to flourish themselves.

Something I have noticed as a fundraiser for the ministry I serve, is that often ministries will hoover up funding as a consequence of their professional charity setup. They know how to fundraise; they have professional fundraisers and for institutional funders they are easier to work with than churches. My worry is that local churches aren't able to access the resources they need to grow. Trusts and Foundations can prefer non-local church-led projects that have clearly defined outcomes and measurable achievements. It is much easier, quicker and arguably more impacting, to work centrally with organizations who work nationally or internationally. Church ministry tends to be slow and messy; this isn't compatible with parameters set out by grant-making foundations. I get these tensions, I live with them and work with them, but friends, we need to esteem the Church and favor her over servant ministries. I'm saying this as a ministry leader. Ministry leaders are under no illusions that they are pastors shepherding a flock, they don't administer the sacraments and neither do they have elders that teach the Word (1 Pet. 5:1-5). Leaders of the Reformation helped define what a true church is. Both Martin Luther[6] and John Calvin[7] agreed on the distinctives of a church: it's the congregation of saints, where the pure preaching of the Word of God is heard and where the sacraments are rightly administered. I think this is helpful for our understanding of Christ's Church especially in this post-modern age.

In Acts 20, before leaving Miletus for Jerusalem, the Apostle Paul assembled the elders of the Ephesian church and gave them some parting words. Emotions were running high all around, both joy and grief at Paul's leaving. Paul had taught the Ephesian church the whole counsel of God. They'd been instructed about how a church should be planted, structured and shepherded. They knew Paul's teaching and experienced the beauty of the local body of believers we call a church. A gathered people, meeting for corporate worship and fellowship, with prayer and singing and the preaching of the Word of God. Pastor Paul addresses his elders with great emotion. Do we have similar emotion or affection within our hearts? Do we as givers really love the Church? Do we have a passionate affection for the Church as we gaze on its beauty set against the darkness of the world? The Church should be treasured by us as she is by God. So we should also belong

---

6   Luther's Augsburg Confession (1530), stated that the Church is 'the congregation of saints, in which the Gospel is rightly taught and the Sacraments are rightly administered' (Article 7). https://bookofconcord.org/augsburg-confession/article-vii/

7   Calvin's Institutes states 'Where we see the Word of God purely preached and heard, where we see the sacraments administered according to Christ's institution, there, it is not to be doubted, the church of God exists.' Calvin's *Institutes*, p. 62 (4.1.9).

to the Church just like the saints in Ephesus. Through our financial gifts, prayer and hard work, we are to strengthen the Church. We do this through our local church.

In Paul's heart we see genuine fellowship, sweetness, joy and love for the Church. How do you feel about the Church? Do you love her? Can you say you have fallen in love with her as Christ has? Perhaps we have grown cold and indifferent about the Church. And so we choose to withhold our giving and put it elsewhere. Sometimes it can be challenging to think of the Church as precious when we get hurt. Let's try to see the Church as God sees her with His eternal perspective. Let's join Paul and the Ephesian elders and be overcome with emotion for the Church. This is why you should prioritize your giving to the local elder-run church.

Allow me to attempt to define what I mean by the Church from the Bible. The New Testament describes the Church as those who have been gathered together from different places and social spheres (1 Cor. 12:13) into a gathered assembly. It's not a building or a place, neither is it a Zoom room or Google Hangout, but it is a community of people called out of the world through faith. Called out of darkness into light. The Church isn't defined by politics, organizational structure or methodology. It's defined by the assembly of the redeemed of Jesus. The Church isn't defined by what we do, but by who we are in Christ. The Church is where God's presence, promises and purposes are known and experienced. We can't say this about a Christian organization. The Church is created by God to delight in Christ and be the object of His love and happiness.

Paul makes this charge to the elders of the church:

> In all things I have shown you that by working hard in this way we must help the weak and remember the words of the Lord Jesus, how he himself said, 'It is more blessed to give than to receive' (Acts 20:35).

John Stott used to say that the pew cannot rise above the pulpit. These are words born out of experience as a seasoned pastor. Cheerful generosity must be modelled by church leadership and through the body. Generosity begins in the assembly of believers not in a conference or retreat. It's the last thing Pastor Paul told these church leaders before he prayed with them and left. This is a poignant reminder to those leading churches and ministries not to hoover up and consume resources but to be a channel of blessing to the weak and needy.

Look, I'm not telling you not to give to people outside of the Church. I've made much of the Church because, in my experience, churches struggle with money, especially in needy neighborhoods where the work is hard and slow. I know Pastors don't find it easy to teach on generosity or talk about money with their congregations. Churches often can't access funds that organizations are able to access. Christians don't tend to be strategic or planned about their giving. So, many churches just don't tend to have a lot of resources for growth, especially if their congregations aren't supporting the work sufficiently. I think there are other good reasons for this cash shortage that have more to do with the vision and leadership of the Church. Churches should always be growing and if they're not then something isn't right! Health produces growth.

Conclusion

By all means, do give to homeless people, help the poor family down the street, help support the University or College you graduated from, support your seminary, bless charities that work with disabled people and donate to the mission agency. Yes, all this of course. I'm fighting the case for givers to have the right priorities, God's priorities. Where do yours lie? Let's allow our hearts to be moved by God's big heart.

> Lord, you love the cheerful giver, who with open heart and hand blesses freely, as a river that refreshes all the land. Grant us then the grace of giving with a spirit large and free, that our life and all our living we may consecrate to thee.
>
> We are thine, thy mercy sought us, found us in death's dreadful way, to the fold in safety brought us, nevermore from thee to stray. Thine own life thou freely gavest as an off'ring on the cross for each sinner whom thou savest from eternal shame and loss.
>
> Blest by thee with gifts and graces, may we heed thy church's call; gladly in all times and places give to thee who givest all. Thou hast bought us, and no longer can we claim to be our own; ever free and ever stronger, we shall serve thee, Lord, alone.
>
> Savior, thou hast freely given all the blessings we enjoy, earthly store and bread of heaven, love and peace without alloy; humbly now we bow before thee, and our all to thee resign; for the kingdom, pow'r, and glory are, O Lord, forever thine (Robert Murray, 1898).[8]

---

8   Robert Murray, Trinity Psalter Hymnal #184.

God promises to fill the whole world with His glory, to make Christ known in all nations, to build His kingdom. All of that is, of course, just the overflow of the big heart of God to the world. But we make God small, we expect small things. God's vision isn't just to maintain a little church building in a little town, but to fill the whole earth with His majestic glory. If money follows vision, then an ocean of financial resources should follow this one! If only Christians would believe that God is accomplishing His big vision today.

Now, friend, you have a decision to make. When I finished writing this book, I had to realign my use of money and property. I had to change the way I viewed what God had entrusted me to steward. The truths that flowed out, hit me front and center of my heart. I hope, for your good and joy, they will do the same for you.

So, what will you do? Will you allow your life to be reformed around the Lord and His Word? You will experience such a radical transformation in your mind and heart, because you share in His life and partake of the divine nature. And if you have God's heart, you simply must take action with what you have, because you'll have a big heart like the triune God. Happy, loving, meek, outpouring and sacrificially giving of Himself. As the Father generously overflows through the Son, who gives the Spirit to be poured out in your heart, so may you overflow the life and love of God to the world.

Acknowledgments

In writing this book, I'm indebted to a few good friends and family. I'm thankful to Dr. Michael Reeves for helping map out the book, one smoky morning near Wheaton, Illinois. Without the enthusiasm and encouragement of Michael Reeves and Daniel Henderson, this book probably wouldn't exist. Thank you, Daniel, for your unwavering support and for telling everyone about this. I'm also grateful to J. Paul. Fridenmaker for your advice and encouragement, you have walked alongside me during this project. I'm deeply thankful to my Pastor, Tom Clewer, for proofreading the manuscript. This is a better book because of your valuable contribution.

I am greatly appreciative of the encouragement I have received from Willie MacKenzie at Christian Focus. I would like to thank Stephen Moore for helping out with some Hebrew translation and other colleagues at Union School of Theology for their help. Finally, I'm thankful to my wife, Hye Lim, for her love and continual support, and for giving me the space to write. I couldn't do it without you!

Also available from Christian Focus Publications...

REVOLU-
TIONARY

GOD

HOW
KNOWING
HIM
CHANGES
EVERYTHING

JOEL MORRIS

978-1-5271-0419-8

Revolutionary God

How Knowing Him Changes Everything

Joel Morris

History is full of revolutions, led by people willing to stand up against oppression and lead a movement. People who embody the heart values of the movement. Jesus wasn't a political or military leader, but he did come to bring the greatest revolution this world has seen. For his fellow revolutionaries, Jesus has paid the greatest price. He brings the most incendiary and divisive message you will ever hear or speak about. Will we follow his lead?

This is a book is a call to spiritual revolution. Each chapter points us to Jesus, the ultimate revolutionary, and shares the testimony of a faithful Christian who lived and 'all in' for Jesus. A short, snappy book that challenges us to go all in for the gospel and reminds us of the power of living a Jesus–centred life.

Mez McConnell
Pastor, Niddrie Community Church and Ministry Director of
20Schemes

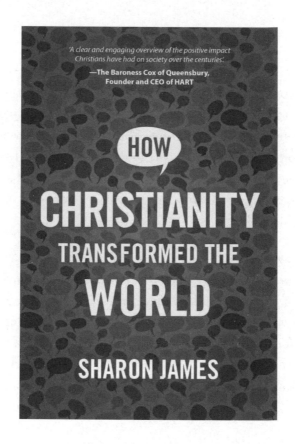

'A clear and engaging overview of the positive impact Christians have had on society over the centuries.'
—The Baroness Cox of Queensbury, Founder and CEO of HART

HOW

CHRISTIANITY

TRANSFORMED THE

WORLD

SHARON JAMES

978-1-5271-0647-5

How Christianity Transformed the World

Sharon James

Many people today would say that Christianity has done more harm than good to our world. Sharon James argues, however, in seeking to love their neighbour and reflect God's moral character the followers of Jesus have had a largely positive impact on our society. James takes a number of areas – education, healthcare, justice, human dignity – and traces the ways in which these benefits have spread with the gospel.

... if you've been influenced to believe that the Christian gospel is a virulent intellectual infection that should be eradicated, that it robs people of joy and freedom, that it oppresses women and makes its heavenly-minded adherents of little earthly good, then you very much need to read this book.

Jon Bloom
President, Desiring God, Minneapolis, Minnesota

... skilfully combines historical research, biblical ethics and contemporary analysis to prove that the gospel really is good news for all people!

Elizabeth McQuoid
Author and commissioning editor, Keswick Ministries

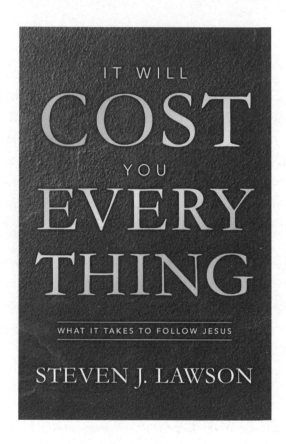

IT WILL

COST

YOU

EVERY

THING

WHAT IT TAKES TO FOLLOW JESUS

STEVEN J. LAWSON

978-1-5271-0703-8

It Will Cost You Everything

What it Takes to Follow Jesus

Steven J. Lawson

Nestled in a few verses in Luke's Gospel is a Jesus who would not have been tolerated today: He was not politically correct and He certainly did not try to save people's feelings. Steven Lawson unpacks these few verses, looking at the unashamed honesty, passion, and urgency with which Jesus explains the life–long cost involved in choosing to follow Him. True Christianity is the biggest sacrifice any person ever makes ... but it is in pursuit of the most precious prize ever glimpsed.

... a book that searches your heart because it exposes you to the holy and compassionate gaze of Jesus Christ.

Joel R. Beeke

President, Puritan Reformed Theological Seminary, Grand Rapids, Michigan

A fickle or indifferent disciple is a contradiction. Here is a book every Christian ought to read and seriously take to heart.

John MacArthur

Chancellor Emeritus, The Master's University and Seminary and Pastor–Teacher, Grace Community Church, Sun Valley, California

Church
For Grown-Ups
INTENTIONAL MATURITY
FOR GOSPEL CONGREGATIONS
John Benton

978-1-5271-0680-2

Church for Grown-Ups

Intentional Maturity for Gospel Congregations

JOHN BENTON

In a self-centred, immature world the Church is called to be different. Christians of all ages should be growing in spiritual maturity. John Benton guides us through what the book of Philippians has to say about a maturing church and gives helpful suggestions for how this can be put into practice and shows the joy that can be ours when we live God's way.

... discipleship means commitment, and commitment involves sacrifice. Paul's deep love for the church is evident throughout Philippians, and John Benton's love for the local church shines through this short book. Real joy comes when we are liberated from the endless and futile quest for self-fulfilment, and give ourselves to Christ and to His people.

Sharon James
Social Policy Analyst, The Christian Institute

What a fabulous book! A must-read for all – not just football fans. Loved it!
- Glenn Hoddle

A GREATER
GLORY
FROM PITCH TO PULPIT

GAVIN PEACOCK

978-1-5271-0679-6

A Greater Glory

From Pitch to Pulpit

GAVIN PEACOCK

What makes a man walk away from his life as a professional footballer turned BBC pundit to become a church minister?

They say it is every schoolboy's dream to play in the F.A. Cup Final and it's a dream that came true for Gavin Peacock. In his riveting autobiography follow Gavin's journey from a child growing up in a footballing family to Chelsea captain; from a son following in his father's footsteps to a husband and father supporting his own family; from pundit to preacher.

What a fabulous book! A must-read for all – not just football fans. I loved working with Gavin as his manager at Chelsea and I've always said he was in my top 3 players I ever signed as a manager. His talent has shone through again in this wonderful book. A beautiful insight to Gavin's life and an inspiration to all. Loved it!

Glenn Hoddle

Former England and Chelsea Manager

As a pastor who would have loved to be a footballer I really enjoyed this book about a footballer who loves being a pastor. A terrific story of someone who has spent his life heading towards the goal to receive a prize that doesn't tarnish with time.

Alistair Begg

Senior Pastor, Parkside Church, Chagrin Falls, Ohio

Christian Focus Publications

Our mission statement —

STAYING FAITHFUL

In dependence upon God we seek to impact the world through literature faithful to His infallible Word, the Bible. Our aim is to ensure that the Lord Jesus Christ is presented as the only hope to obtain forgiveness of sin, live a useful life and look forward to heaven with Him.

Our books are published in four imprints:

CHRISTIAN
FOCUS

Popular works including biographies, commentaries, basic doctrine and Christian living.

CHRISTIAN
HERITAGE

Books representing some of the best material from the rich heritage of the church.

MENTOR

Books written at a level suitable for Bible College and seminary students, pastors, and other serious readers. The imprint includes commentaries, doctrinal studies, examination of current issues and church history.

CF4•K

Children's books for quality Bible teaching and for all age groups: Sunday school curriculum, puzzle and activity books; personal and family devotional titles, biographies and inspirational stories — because you are never too young to know Jesus!

Christian Focus Publications Ltd,
Geanies House, Fearn, Ross-shire,
IV20 1TW, Scotland, United Kingdom.
www.christianfocus.com